THE NEW ORLEANS SAINTS STORY:

THE 43-YEAR ROAD TO THE SUPER BOWL XLIV CHAMPIONSHIP

Dan Fathow

Megalodon Entertainment, LLC.

Published by Megalodon Entertainment, LLC. (USA)
www.MegalodonEntertainment.com

First Printing: February 2010

Copyright © 2010 Megalodon Entertainment LLC. All rights reserved.

All rights reserved under the International and Pan-American Copyright conventions. No part of this publication may be reproduced, or transmitted by any means in any form (electronic, photocopying, mechanical, recording, or any other method), without the specific written permission of the publisher. Please, direct questions to info@megalodonentertainment.com.

Printed in the United States of America.

ISBN: 978-0-9800605-7-7
ISBN-10: 0-9800605-7-5

The NFL, Super Bowl, Monday Night Football, and all team names are ™ of The National Football League, NFL Productions LLC., NFL Enterprises LLC., or their respective teams. No affiliation to any of them is claimed or implied by this publication.

BULK INQUERIES:
Quantity discounts are available on bulk orders of this novel for educational, fund-raising, promotional, and special sales purposes. For details, please contact www.MegalodonEntertainment.com

CHECK OUT ANOTHER NEW ORLEANS ORIGINAL

FROM LEWIS ALEMAN,
BESTSELLING AUTHOR OF COLD STREAK
A 20-YEAR RACE THROUGH TIME...

IF YOU COULD GO BACK IN TIME, WHO WOULD YOU SAVE?

"There is craftsmanship in Aleman's details; elaborate use of adjectival simile and metaphor ... stimulates ... memorable ... space-time research well done"
Dionne Charlet
Where Y'At Magazine
Feb 2010

"*Faces in Time* was an adventurous, fast paced, time traveling novel...loved the twists and turns...Lewis writes beautifully, his work is filled with great detailed descriptions...a great adventure. I haven't seen anything out like it."
La Femme Readers
December 12, 2009

WWW.LEWISALEMAN.COM
MYSPACE.COM/LEWISALEMAN
YOUTUBE.COM/LEWISALEMAN

Check out more Great Releases from

Megalodon Entertainment LLC

An Amazon Bestseller
#1 in Myspace Books
A Kindle Bestseller

Cold Streak
Lewis Aleman

"An enthralling story of vengeance, 'Cold Streak' is deftly written and a must for thriller fans..."
Midwest Book Review

"Lewis's hold-your-breath style of descriptive writing will keep you swimming in his creative vocabulary for hours...multi-layered metaphors...elaborate prose..." *Alex Hutchinson, Blogcritics*

Enter Laura's World...
Her family is brutally murdered, and she finds herself on her knees praying for things she never could have imagined. Her dark journey of revenge takes off as she hunts her family's killers, while being chased down by a troubled detective, his lovelorn partner, and an inner voice that grants her no peace. Her quest lures her through an explosive music scene, down unlit alleyways, to the edge of a towering church rooftop, and into the nightmarish landscape of her own mind. Will she get her justice before time runs out? Will her own lust for vengeance consume all that is left of her in the process?

www.LewisAleman.com

Table of Contents

Part I: 43 Years of History 3

How It All Began.. 3
1967 4
1968 5
1969 6
1970 7
1971 9
1972 10
1973 11
1974 12
1975 13
1976 14
1977 15
1978 16
1979 17
1980 18
1981 19
1982 20
1983 22
1984 23
1985 24
1986 26
1987 27
1988 28
1989 30
1990 32
1991 33
1992 35
1993 37
1994 39
1995 42
1996 43
1997 45
1998 48
1999 50
2000 52
2001 54

2002 56
2003 58
2004 59
2005 60
2006 63
2007 65
2008 67
2009 68

PART II: 2009 THE DREAM SEASON . 71

Week 1   vs. Detroit Lions............................. 73
Week 2   vs. Philadelphia Eagles................... 74
Week 3   vs. Buffalo Bills 75
Week 4   vs. New York Jets 76
Week 5   vs. BYE 78
Week 6   vs. New York Giants 78
Week 7   vs. Miami Dolphins....................... 79
Week 8   vs. Atlanta Falcons 81
Week 9   vs. Carolina Panthers..................... 82
Week 10 vs. St. Louis Rams.......................... 84
Week 11 vs. Tampa Bay Buccaneers 85
Week 12 vs. New England Patriots. 86
Week 13 vs. Washington Redskins 88
Week 14 vs. Atlanta Falcons. 89
Week 15 vs. Dallas Cowboys........................ 90
Week 16 vs. Tampa Bay Buccaneers 92
Week 17 vs. Carolina Panthers..................... 94
Week 18 vs. Playoffs Wild Card BYE 95
Week 19 vs. NFC Divisional Round 95
Week 20 vs. NFC Championship Game....... 97
Week 21 vs. Super Bowl XLIV..................... 99

PART III: SPECIAL LOOKS..................... 107

Jim Finks 109
Buddy Diliberto... 111
Saints Coaches Stats & Comparison 115
Saints Quarterbacks Stats & Comparison... 119

Part I:
43 Years of History

The journey for the New Orleans Saints to reach the big game started a long 43 years before finally earning their ticket to Super Bowl XLIV on February the 7th 2010 in Miami, FL.

A cynic could sum up the Saints 4-plus decade history in a glib little string of words:

> "27 Losing Seasons, 6 Even Seasons,
> and only 10 Winning Seasons."

But, that short statement, while statistically accurate, misses out on years of struggle, years of loyalty, and years of a city facing the hardships of poverty, racial tension, and natural disasters. It ignores songs and signs proclaiming, "Bless You Boys," "The Dome Patrol," and "I Believe." And most certainly, it misses out on the joy in every true Saints fan who has waited his entire life to see his beloved Black and Gold make it to the Super Bowl.

How It All Began...

The Saints began as an expansion team in 1967, and are named after the famous jazz tune, "When the Saints Come Marching In," which is forever linked to the city of New Orleans. In typical New Orleans political fashion, the decision to bring an NFL team to the city was the result of a backroom deal between Pete Rozelle, the then-current NFL commissioner, and Hale Boggs, House Representative (D) from Louisiana, who also served as a Majority Whip and Majority Leader. Despite the shady negotiating, there were legitimate and impressive reasons to bring an NFL franchise to the Crescent City. New Orleans had hosted record crowds at NFL games in Tulane stadium, proving that the city had viable crowd support. Couple that with the city's built-in tourism attractions of The French Quarter and Mardi Gras, and bringing pro football to New Orleans seemed to be a no-brainer. One would have to wonder why any suspicious meetings would

The New Orleans Saints Story 4

be necessary since New Orleans appeared to be a perfect place to birth a new NFL team. Since Hale Boggs died in a mysterious plane crash over Alaska in 1972 and Rozelle died of brain cancer in 1996, we may never know exactly what was discussed in secret or if any shenanigans took place. What is often speculated is that Boggs promised to back the NFL in monopoly charges being brought against it in return for Boggs's home state receiving an NFL franchise.

Coincidentally, the official announcement of New Orleans being selected to receive an NFL expansion team came on November 1, 1966, a Catholic holiday called All Saints' Day, which is even more fitting considering New Orleans has a large Catholic population.

The original team owner was oil tycoon, John W. Mecom Jr., who hired the Atlanta Falcons' offensive coordinator Tom Fears to be the Saints' first head coach.

1967 - THE FIRST SEASON

The Saints' first season in 1967 started off with a bang against the Los Angeles Rams with its very first play being a 94-yard kickoff return for a touchdown by John Gilliam in Tulane Stadium. Gilliam, who went on to play in two Super Bowls with the Vikings and was named a Pro Bowl player, was the first player to score a touchdown as a Saint. Unfortunately, the Saints lost the game 27-13.

One of the highlights of the year was the unexpected performance from rookie wide receiver Danny Abramowicz, who was only a 17th round draft pick. Abramowicz was the team leader in receiving yards with 721 yards on 50 catches with 6 touchdowns.

Quarterback duties were split between Billy Kilmer and Gary Cuozzo. Unfortunately, despite the efforts of both men, the Saints did not earn their first win until Week 8 of the season.

The first year was a trying one for the Saints, as can be expected with any expansion team, but their 3-11 record, while unimpressive, was still the best record for any NFL expansion team at that time. So while the future presented challenges and demanded improvement, the outlook was hopeful as no other NFL expansion team had started off so well. In the least, the Saints appeared to be on the right track.

1967

Week	Date	Opponent	Score
1	17-Sep	Rams	L 13-27
2	24-Sep	Redskins	L 10-30
3	1-Oct	Browns	L 7-42
4	8-Oct	Giants	L 21-27
5	15-Oct	Cowboys	L 10-14
6	22-Oct	49ers	L 13-27
7	29-Oct	Steelers	L 10-14
8	5-Nov	Eagles	W 31-24
9	12-Nov	Cowboys	L 10-27
10	19-Nov	Eagles	L 28-41
11	26-Nov	Falcons	W 27-24
12	3-Dec	Cardinals	L 20-31
13	10-Dec	Colts	L 10-30
14	17-Dec	Redskins	W 30-14

1968 – 2ND SEASON

The second season for the Saints showed some modest improvement. Danny Abramowicz once again led the team in receiving yards, this time with 890 yards on 54 catches for 7 touchdowns, averaging 16.5 yards per catch. Billy Kilmer earned the starting quarterback position, completing 54% of his passes for 2,060 yards and 15 touchdowns. The Saints also had a Pro Bowl player in Dave Rowe who played defensive tackle.

The New Orleans Saints Story 6

The Saints' record for the year was 4-9 with 1 tie. While it may seem abysmal, it was the best record for a 2nd-year expansion team at that time.

1968

Week	Date	Opponent	Score
1	15-Sep-68	Cleveland Browns	L 24-10
2	22-Sep-68	Washington Redskins	W 37-17
3	29-Sep-68	St. Louis Cardinals	L 21-20
4	6-Oct-68	at New York Giants	L 38-21
5	13-Oct-68	Minnesota Vikings	W 20-17
6	20-Oct-68	at Pittsburgh Steelers	W 16-12
7	27-Oct-68	at St. Louis Cardinals	L 31-17
8	3-Nov-68	Dallas Cowboys	L 17-3
9	10-Nov-68	at Cleveland Browns	L 35-17
10	17-Nov-68	at Green Bay Packers	L 29-7
11	24-Nov-68	at Detroit Lions	T 20-20
12	1-Dec-68	Chicago Bears	L 23-17
13	8-Dec-68	at Philadelphia Eagles	L 29-17
14	15-Dec-68	Pittsburgh Steelers	W 24-14

1969 – 3RD SEASON

The Saints improved their record to 5-9. Danny Abramowicz caught for 1,015 yards on 73 catches averaging 13.9 yards per grab. Abramowicz also led the NFL in receptions, and was 3rd in the league for receiving yards. Quarterback Billy Gilbreath completed 193 of 360 passes for a 54% completion ratio.

Making it to the Pro Bowl were Saints players Tom Dempsey (#19 Kicker), Tony Baker (#38 FB), Andy Livingston (#48 HB), and Jake Kupp (#50 OG).

History 7

While the Saints' record still seems poor, the Saints' 3-year win-loss record was the best produced by any expansion team to date.

1969

Week	Date	Opponent	Score
1	21-Sep-69	Washington Redskins	L 26-20
2	28-Sep-69	Dallas Cowboys	L 21-17
3	5-Oct-69	at Los Angeles Rams	L 36-17
4	12-Oct-69	Cleveland Browns	L 27-17
5	19-Oct-69	Baltimore Colts	L 30-10
6	26-Oct-69	at Philadelphia Eagles	L 13-10
7	2-Nov-69	at St. Louis Cardinals	W 51-42
8	9-Nov-69	at Dallas Cowboys	L 33-17
9	16-Nov-69	at New York Giants	W 25-24
10	23-Nov-69	San Francisco 49ers	W 43-38
11	30-Nov-69	Philadelphia Eagles	W 26-17
12	7-Dec-69	at Atlanta Falcons	L 45-17
13	14-Dec-69	at Washington Redskins	L 17-14
14	21-Dec-69	Pittsburgh Steelers	W 27-24

1970 – 4TH SEASON

While there was a footnote for all 3 of the previous seasons in that the Saints had done better than any expansion team in that given year, 1970 was an utter disaster with the Saints finishing up with 2 wins, 11 losses, and 1 tie.

The ray of light in this dark season was certainly kicker Tom Dempsey's 63-yard field goal to beat the Detroit Lions in the last second of the game. The gargantuan field goal took place before a home crowd in Tulane Stadium.

The New Orleans Saints Story 8

Dempsey described the record-breaking field goal, "When I lined up to kick my record-setting 63-yard field goal in 1970, we had the ball in the closed-in area of Tulane Stadium. The winds in that stadium sometimes would swirl and push balls wide to the left or wide to the right. The stadium was shaped like a big horseshoe, open at one end of the stadium and closed at the other. When it got windy, it was difficult to judge what was going to happen to the ball once it was kicked. But I got a good snap and a good hold, and I knew I had hit it well enough to go the distance. Considering that stadium, though, the question of whether the ball would stay straight was in the back of my mind. My snapper was Jackie Burkett and my holder was Joe Scarpati. It's important to have a good holder. Everything was perfect for me that day: I got a perfect snap, I got a perfect hold, and I got a lot of protection. No one ever accomplishes anything alone in football. We all like to think that we can, but that's just not true. It's always been a team game, always will be. So everything went well, and everyone else did their job. The last thing was for me to try to do mine. I thought I kicked it pretty well--I thought it had a chance. I was hoping the winds wouldn't swirl and drive the ball off-course. It seemed like it took forever to get there. I just kept watching it, wondering if it had enough distance. Finally, the referees raised their hands that it was good." (http://www.mmbolding.com/BSR/Longest_Field_Goal_in_NFL_History.htm)

Dempsey's record has still never been beaten. After 28 years, Jason Elam of the Denver Broncos managed to tie it on October 25th, 1998, in a game against Jacksonville.

At midseason, Tom Fears was replaced as head coach by J.D. Roberts.

Danny Abramowicz was once again the team's leading receiver with 906 yards on 55 catches for an average of 16.5 yards per reception.

1970

Week	Date	Opponent	Score
1	20-Sep-70	Atlanta Falcons	L 14-3
2	27-Sep-70	at Minnesota Vikings	L 26-0

History 9

3	4-Oct-70	New York Giants	W 14-10
4	11-Oct-70	at St. Louis Cardinals	L 24-17
5	18-Oct-70	at San Francisco 49ers	T 20-20
6	25-Oct-70	at Atlanta Falcons	L 32-14
7	1-Nov-70	Los Angeles Rams	L 30-17
8	8-Nov-70	Detroit Lions	W 19-17
9	15-Nov-70	at Miami Dolphins	L 21-10
10	22-Nov-70	Denver Broncos	L 31-6
11	29-Nov-70	at Cincinnati Bengals	L 26-6
12	6-Dec-70	at Los Angeles Rams	L 34-16
13	13-Dec-70	San Francisco 49ers	L 38-27
14	20-Dec-70	Chicago Bears	L 24-3

1971 – 5th Season

The most notable change for the 1971 Season was the 1st-Round 2nd-Overall pick of Archie Manning, an All-American quarterback from Ole Miss. Manning was in the running for the Heisman trophy during his senior year, having passed for over 5,700 yards and 56 touchdowns over his college career.

During his rookie season with the Saints, Manning threw for 1,164 yards on 86 of 177 pass attempts with 6 touchdowns and 9 interceptions for a 48.6 completion ratio. He was sacked a league-leading 40 times.

During the year, the Saints had 2 huge upsets over the Los Angeles Rams and the Super Bowl Champion Dallas Cowboys, with Manning rushing for 3 touchdowns over both games. Sadly, the Saints could only win two more games besides the upsets, finishing the year with a 4-8-2 record.

1971

Week	Date	Opponent	Score

The New Orleans Saints Story 10

1	19-Sep-71	Los Angeles Rams	W 24-20
2	26-Sep-71	San Francisco 49ers	L 38-20
3	3-Oct-71	at Houston Oilers	T 13-13
4	10-Oct-71	at Chicago Bears	L 35-14
5	17-Oct-71	Dallas Cowboys	W 24-14
6	24-Oct-71	at Atlanta Falcons	L 28-6
7	31-Oct-71	at Washington Redskins	L 24-14
8	7-Nov-71	Oakland Raiders	T 21-21
9	14-Nov-71	at San Francisco 49ers	W 26-20
10	21-Nov-71	Minnesota Vikings	L 23-10
11	28-Nov-71	at Green Bay Packers	W 29-21
12	5-Dec-71	at Los Angeles Rams	L 45-28
13	12-Dec-71	Cleveland Browns	L 21-17
14	19-Dec-71	Atlanta Falcons	L 24-20

1972 – 6TH SEASON

The Saints went 1-11, despite a decent season from Archie Manning. Manning's numbers were 51% completions on 448 attempts for 2,781 yards with 18 TDs and 21 interceptions. Keeping in mind that he accomplished this on a team that only managed to win one game during the whole season, Manning performed well with what we had to work with. To further put things into perspective, team rushing leader, Bob Gresham, rushed for 381 yards, and Manning was right behind him with 351 rushing yards of his own. Manning led the league in completions and pass attempts while also being the most sacked quarterback at 43 times.

1972 marked the Saints' first Monday Night Football game, which they lost to the Kansas City Chiefs by the score of 17-20.

1972

History 11

Week	Date	Opponent	Score
1	17-Sep-72	at Los Angeles Rams	L 34-14
2	25-Sep-72	Kansas City Chiefs	L 20-17
3	1-Oct-72	San Francisco 49ers	L 37-2
4	8-Oct-72	at New York Giants	L 45-21
5	15-Oct-72	Atlanta Falcons	L 21-14
6	22-Oct-72	at San Francisco 49ers	T 20-20
7	29-Oct-72	Philadelphia Eagles	W 21-3
8	5-Nov-72	at Minnesota Vikings	L 37-6
9	12-Nov-72	at Atlanta Falcons	L 36-20
10	19-Nov-72	at Detroit Lions	L 27-14
11	26-Nov-72	Los Angeles Rams	W 19-16
12	3-Dec-72	at New York Jets	L 18-17
13	10-Dec-72	New England Patriots	L 17-10
14	17-Dec-72	Green Bay Packers	L 30-20

1973 – 7TH SEASON

1973 was a slightly better year for the Black and Gold with 5 wins and 9 losses. New coach John North took over, but the Saints started the year horribly by losing to Atlanta 62-7. The year also marked the Saints' second loss on Monday Night Football, this time to the Dallas Cowboys by a score of 40-3.

Archie Manning threw for 1,642 yards on 140 of 367 pass attempts with 10 touchdowns and 12 interceptions for a 52.4 completion ratio.

On a positive note, the Saints' defense held O.J. Simpson to just 79 yards in a year that Simpson rushed for over 2,000 yards.

1973

Week	Date	Opponent	Score

The New Orleans Saints Story 12

1	16-Sep-73	Atlanta Falcons	L 62-7
2	24-Sep-73	at Dallas Cowboys	L 40-3
3	30-Sep-73	at Baltimore Colts	L 14-10
4	7-Oct-73	Chicago Bears	W 21-6
5	14-Oct-73	Detroit Lions	W 20-13
6	21-Oct-73	at San Francisco 49ers	L 40-0
7	28-Oct-73	Washington Redskins	W 19-3
8	4-Nov-73	Buffalo Bills	W 13-0
9	11-Nov-73	at Los Angeles Rams	L 29-7
10	18-Nov-73	at San Diego Chargers	L 17-14
11	25-Nov-73	Los Angeles Rams	L 24-13
12	2-Dec-73	at Green Bay Packers	L 30-10
13	9-Dec-73	San Francisco 49ers	W 16-10
14	16-Dec-73	at Atlanta Falcons	L 14-10

<u>1974 – 8th Season</u>

Just like the previous year, the Saints ended the season at 5-9. The Saints scored 20 or more points in only 2 games during the entire year.

One of the few positive notes of this year was Alvin Maxson's rookie season of rushing 714 yards on 165 carries, averaging 4.33 yards per carry.

Manning threw for 1,429 yards on 134 of 261 pass attempts with 6 touchdowns and 16 interceptions for a 51.3 completion ratio.

1974

Week	Date	Opponent	Score
1	15-Sep-74	San Francisco 49ers	L 17-13
2	22-Sep-74	at Los Angeles Rams	L 24-0
3	29-Sep-74	Atlanta Falcons	W 14-13

History 13

4	6-Oct-74	at Chicago Bears	L 24-10
5	13-Oct-74	at Denver Broncos	L 33-17
6	20-Oct-74	at Atlanta Falcons	W 13-3
7	27-Oct-74	Philadelphia Eagles	W 14-10
8	3-Nov-74	at Detroit Lions	L 19-14
9	10-Nov-74	Miami Dolphins	L 21-0
10	17-Nov-74	Los Angeles Rams	W 20-7
11	25-Nov-74	Pittsburgh Steelers	L 28-7
12	1-Dec-74	at Minnesota Vikings	L 29-9
13	8-Dec-74	St. Louis Cardinals	W 14-0
14	15-Dec-74	at San Francisco 49ers	L 35-21

1975 – 9th Season

The Saints finally began play at the freshly constructed Superdome. Unfortunately, the inaugural game left the Saints completely shutout 21-0 by the Cincinnati Bengals.

John North was replaced as head coach during the season with Hefferle filling in. The year ended with the Saints having only 2 wins and 12 losses.

Manning threw for 1,683 yards on 159 of 338 pass attempts with 7 touchdowns and 20 interceptions for a 47.0 completion ratio. It was not an accurate year for Manning, having thrown nearly 3 times as many touchdowns as interceptions.

1975

Week	Date	Opponent	Score
1	21-Sep-75	at Washington Redskins	L 41-3
2	28-Sep-75	Cincinnati Bengals	L 21-0
3	5-Oct-75	at Atlanta Falcons	L 14-7
4	12-Oct-75	Green Bay Packers	W 20-19
5	19-Oct-75	at San Francisco 49ers	L 35-21

6	26-Oct-75	at Los Angeles Rams	L 38-14
7	2-Nov-75	Atlanta Falcons	W 23-7
8	9-Nov-75	at Oakland Raiders	L 48-10
9	16-Nov-75	Minnesota Vikings	L 20-7
10	23-Nov-75	San Francisco 49ers	L 16-6
11	30-Nov-75	at Cleveland Browns	L 17-16
12	7-Dec-75	Los Angeles Rams	L 14-7
13	14-Dec-75	at New York Giants	L 28-14
14	21-Dec-75	Chicago Bears	L 42-17

1976 – 10TH SEASON

Hank Stram took over the reigns as head coach, but Archie Manning was out the entire season due to a shoulder injury.

Running backs Chuck Muncie and Tony Galbreath were called Thunder and Lightning and provided some excitement for Saints' fans, but the team couldn't muster many wins, going 4-10.

1976

Week	Date	Opponent	Score
1	12-Sep-76	Minnesota Vikings	L 40-9
2	19-Sep-76	Dallas Cowboys	L 24-6
3	26-Sep-76	at Kansas City Chiefs	W 27-17
4	3-Oct-76	Houston Oilers	L 31-26
5	10-Oct-76	Atlanta Falcons	W 30-0
6	17-Oct-76	at San Francisco 49ers	L 33-3
7	24-Oct-76	Los Angeles Rams	L 16-10
8	31-Oct-76	at Atlanta Falcons	L 23-20
9	7-Nov-76	at Green Bay Packers	L 32-27
10	14-Nov-76	Detroit Lions	W 17-16

History 15

11	21-Nov-76	at Seattle Seahawks	W 51-27
12	28-Nov-76	at Los Angeles Rams	L 33-14
13	5-Dec-76	at New England Patriots	L 27-6
14	12-Dec-76	San Francisco 49ers	L 27-7

1977 – 11TH SEASON

The Saints take a step backward and go 3-11 on the year. One of the only joys for Saints fans this year came with a 42-24 victory over the Chicago Bears in which Archie Manning rushed for 3 touchdowns.

The other rare pleasure during this season was the performance of running back Chuck Muncie, who in his only second season, rushed on 201 carries for 811 yards, averaging 4.03 yards per carry. Muncie's Thunder and Lighting partner, Tony Galbreath, rushed on 168 carries for 644 yards, averaging 3.83 yards per carry. Thunder and Lightning combined for a ground attack of 1,455 yards.

Manning only played in 9 games and threw for 1,284 yards on 113 of 205 pass attempts for 8 touchdowns and 9 interceptions for a 55.1 completion ratio.

1977

Week	Date	Opponent	Score
1	18-Sep-77	Green Bay Packers	L 24-20
2	25-Sep-77	at Detroit Lions	L 23-19
3	2-Oct-77	at Chicago Bears	W 42-24
4	9-Oct-77	San Diego Chargers	L 14-0
5	16-Oct-77	at Los Angeles Rams	L 14-7
6	23-Oct-77	at St. Louis Cardinals	L 49-31
7	30-Oct-77	Los Angeles Rams	W 27-26

The New Orleans Saints Story 16

8	6-Nov-77	at Philadelphia Eagles	L 28-7
9	13-Nov-77	San Francisco 49ers	L 10-7
10	20-Nov-77	Atlanta Falcons	W 21-20
11	27-Nov-77	at San Francisco 49ers	L 20-17
12	4-Dec-77	New York Jets	L 16-13
13	11-Dec-77	Tampa Bay Buccaneers	L 33-14
14	18-Dec-77	at Atlanta Falcons	L 35-7

1978 – 12TH SEASON

Dick Nolan was the new head coach, and he brought the Saints to their first 7-win season, finishing 7-9. While still not a winning season, it was their best to date.

To give Archie Manning some tools to work with, Wes Chandler (receiver) and Conrad Dobler (offensive guard) were brought into the fold. With the new changes, Manning was voted into the Pro Bowl and picked as NFL Man of the Year. His completion ratio was an astounding 61.8% of 471 throws for 3,416 yards, 17 touchdowns, and 16 interceptions.

1978

Week	Date	Opponent	Score
1	3-Sep-78	Minnesota Vikings	W 31-24
2	10-Sep-78	at Green Bay Packers	L 28-17
3	17-Sep-78	Philadelphia Eagles	L 24-17
4	24-Sep-78	at Cincinnati Bengals	W 20-18
5	1-Oct-78	Los Angeles Rams	L 26-20
6	8-Oct-78	Cleveland Browns	L 24-16
7	15-Oct-78	at San Francisco 49ers	W 14-7
8	22-Oct-78	at Los Angeles Rams	W 10-3
9	29-Oct-78	New York Giants	W 28-17
10	5-Nov-78	at Pittsburgh Steelers	L 20-14

11	12-Nov-78	Atlanta Falcons	L 20-17
12	19-Nov-78	at Dallas Cowboys	L 27-7
13	26-Nov-78	at Atlanta Falcons	L 20-17
14	3-Dec-78	San Francisco 49ers	W 24-13
15	10-Dec-78	Houston Oilers	L 17-12
16	17-Dec-78	at Tampa Bay Buccaneers	W 17-10

1979 – 13ᵗʰ Season

The first non-losing season in franchise history! The Saints went 8-8, still under the guidance of head coach Dick Nolan. It didn't bode well when the Saints started the year 0-3, but they finished the year by winning 8 of their remaining 13 games.

1979 was the first season that the Saints had legitimate playoff hopes late in the season. Another highlight was Archie Manning earning his second Pro Bowl trip on his 60% completion ratio for 3,169 yards, 15 touchdowns, 20 interceptions. Henry Childs also went to the Pro Bowl with 846 yards on 51 catches for 16.59 yards per catch. What about Thunder and Lightning? They went to the Pro Bowl too. Chuck Muncie had an amazing year by putting up 1,198 yards with a best-in-league 5.0 yards per carry, and in the process he became the first Saint to rush for over 1,000 yards. Tony Galbreath rushed for 708 yards.

4 Saints' players in the Pro Bowl and the first non-losing season? Not a bad year for the Black and Gold fans.

1979

Week	Date	Opponent	Score
1	2-Sep-79	Atlanta Falcons	L 40-34
2	9-Sep-79	at Green Bay Packers	L 28-19

The New Orleans Saints Story 18

3	16-Sep-79	Philadelphia Eagles	L 26-14
4	23-Sep-79	at San Francisco 49ers	W 30-21
5	30-Sep-79	New York Giants	W 24-14
6	7-Oct-79	Los Angeles Rams	L 35-17
7	14-Oct-79	at Tampa Bay Buccaneers	W 42-14
8	21-Oct-79	Detroit Lions	W 17-7
9	28-Oct-79	at Washington Redskins	W 14-10
10	4-Nov-79	at Denver Broncos	L 10-3
11	11-Nov-79	San Francisco 49ers	W 31-20
12	18-Nov-79	at Seattle Seahawks	L 38-24
13	25-Nov-79	at Atlanta Falcons	W 37-6
14	3-Dec-79	Oakland Raiders	L 42-35
15	9-Dec-79	San Diego Chargers	L 35-0
16	16-Dec-79	at Los Angeles Rams	W 29-14

1980 – 14th Season

Disappointment is not a strong enough word to describe the torture that the 1980 season was for Saints' fans. The Saints were coming off their best season to date, narrowly missing the playoffs, and having sent 4 players to the Pro Bowl. Surely, no one was expecting a 1-15 season, the worst record in franchise history.

Immediately following his 1,000-plus yard season, Chuck Muncie was traded to San Diego. The team's leading rusher, rookie Jim Rodgers, only had a meager 366 yards on 80 carries, averaging 4.57 yards per carry. To put it into perspective, the team's leading rusher barely put up 1/3 of Muncie's numbers from just the year before.

The only bright spots were Wes Chandler receiving for 975 yards on 65 catches, and Archie Manning's 309 completions

History 19

on 509 attempts for 61% completion ratio and 3,716 yards with 23 touchdowns and 20 interceptions. The 3,716 yards were the highest in the NFC that season, and he accomplished this while being sacked 41 times.

Dick Nolan, the man who had turned the Saints around was fired and succeeded by Dick Stanfil.

1980

Week	Date	Opponent	Score
1	7-Sep-80	San Francisco 49ers	L 26-23
2	14-Sep-80	at Chicago Bears	L 22-3
3	21-Sep-80	Buffalo Bills	L 35-26
4	28-Sep-80	at Miami Dolphins	L 21-16
5	5-Oct-80	St. Louis Cardinals	L 40-7
6	12-Oct-80	at Detroit Lions	L 24-13
7	19-Oct-80	Atlanta Falcons	L 41-14
8	26-Oct-80	at Washington Redskins	L 22-14
9	2-Nov-80	at Los Angeles Rams	L 45-31
10	9-Nov-80	Philadelphia Eagles	L 34-21
11	16-Nov-80	at Atlanta Falcons	L 31-13
12	24-Nov-80	Los Angeles Rams	L 27-7
13	30-Nov-80	Minnesota Vikings	L 23-20
14	7-Dec-80	at San Francisco 49ers	L 38-35
15	14-Dec-80	at New York Jets	W 21-20
16	21-Dec-80	New England Patriots	L 38-27

1981 – 15TH SEASON

A little bit better. Under new head coach Bum Phillips, the team goes 4-12. Bum Phillips had previously achieved great success with the Houston Oilers having gone to the playoffs 3

The New Orleans Saints Story 20

years in a row, and going to the AFC Championship game in 2 of them.

Phillips tried to reinvigorate the Saints' offense by using his first round draft pick to acquire Earl Campbell, a Heisman Trophy winner. Campbell did not disappoint and rushed for 1,674 yards, which was an NFL rookie record. The other most notable draft pick and future 2010 Hall of Fame inductee was Rickey Jackson, who provided 8 sacks in his rookie year with the Saints. Also notable to Saints' fans, Hokie Gajan, future New Orleans Saints radio personality, was drafted in the 10th round.

Part of the season's lack of wins can probably be attributed to Archie Manning's limited play resulting from injury.

1981

Week	Date	Opponent	Score
1	6-Sep-81	at Atlanta Falcons	L 27-0
2	13-Sep-81	Los Angeles Rams	W 23-17
3	20-Sep-81	at New York Giants	L 20-7
4	27-Sep-81	at San Francisco 49ers	L 21-14
5	4-Oct-81	Pittsburgh Steelers	L 20-6
6	11-Oct-81	Philadelphia Eagles	L 31-14
7	18-Oct-81	at Cleveland Browns	L 20-17
8	25-Oct-81	Cincinnati Bengals	W 17-7
9	1-Nov-81	Atlanta Falcons	L 41-10
10	8-Nov-81	at Los Angeles Rams	W 21-13
11	15-Nov-81	at Minnesota Vikings	L 20-10
12	22-Nov-81	at Houston Oilers	W 27-24
13	29-Nov-81	Tampa Bay Buccaneers	L 31-14
14	6-Dec-81	at St. Louis Cardinals	L 30-3
15	13-Dec-81	Green Bay Packers	L 35-7
16	20-Dec-81	San Francisco 49ers	L 21-17

1982 – 16TH SEASON

History 21

1982 was a step in the right direction for the Saints, mustering a 4-5 record (the season was cut short due to a strike).

The off-season sucker punched the Saints, leaving a black eye of drug use allegations on Dave Waymer, George Rodgers, Monte Bennent, and ex-Saint Mike Strachan.

The season opener marked the last appearance of Archie Manning in a Saints uniform. He went 1 for 7 with 2 interceptions. Another catastrophe in the season opener was rookie kicker Morten Andersen getting injured on a hit during his very first play, taking him completely off the field for another 8 weeks.

Shortly after the season opener, Archie Manning was traded to the Houston Oilers.

When starting quarterback Dave Wilson was injured, Phillips signed Kenny Stabler who had been released. Stabler did produce good numbers in 1982 with a 61.9% completion ratio on 189 passes for 1,343 yards (keep in mind, there were only 9 games in 1982) with 6 touchdowns and 10 interceptions.

At 4 games into the season, the Saints had a 3-1 record, which was their best record to date. Unfortunately, they would lose 4 of their last 5 games, taking themselves out of postseason contention.

The defense played well, producing 33 sacks in just 9 games.

1982

Week	Date	Opponent	Score
1	12-Sep-82	St. Louis Cardinals	L 21-7
2	19-Sep-82	at Chicago Bears	W 10-0
3	21-Nov-82	Kansas City Chiefs	W 27-17
4	28-Nov-82	at San Francisco 49ers	W 23-20
5	5-Dec-82	Tampa Bay Buccaneers	L 13-10
6	12-Dec-82	at Atlanta Falcons	L 35-0
7	19-Dec-82	at Dallas Cowboys	L 21-7
8	26-Dec-82	Washington Redskins	L 27-10

The New Orleans Saints Story 22

| 9 | 2-Jan-83 | Atlanta Falcons | W 35-6 |

* Strike year

1983 – 17ᵗʰ Season

The Saints achieved a non-losing season of 8-8, which is a vast improvement over 1980's 1-15 showing. Bringing a team from 1-15 to 8-8 in 3 years' time is a notable achievement for Phillips. The Saints had legitimate playoff hopes for the length of the season.

In a game versus the Chicago Bears, Morten Andersen gave the Saints their first overtime win with a 41-yard field goal.

At 5 games into the season, the Saints had a 4-1 record, which was their best start to date.

On December 3rd, 1983, in a game versus the New England Patriots, Morten Andersen kicked a 52-yard field goal to send the game into overtime, and then he kicked a second field goal to win the game for the Saints. Andersen consistently kicking winning field goals would become a familiar sight for Saints fans.

In the last game of the season, the Saints faced off against the Los Angeles Rams. The winner would head to the playoffs in a wild card game, and the loser would get an early start on the off-season. The Saints were up 24-23 over the Rams late in the 4th quarter, closer to the playoffs than they had ever been. With the choice of attempting a 49-yard Morten Andersen field goal or punting, Phillips decided to punt. The Rams scored their only offensive points of the game to beat the Saints, crushing the Black and Gold playoff hopes.

In retrospect, it seems a ridiculous decision to not trust the sure foot of Andersen to extend one's lead with a 49-point field goal, but this was before Andersen had proven himself by hitting kicks just like this year after year. That one decision might have cost the Saints not only their first playoff appearance, but also their first winning season.

1983

Week	Date	Opponent	Score
1	4-Sep-83	St. Louis Cardinals	W 28-17
2	11-Sep-83	at Los Angeles Rams	L 30-27
3	18-Sep-83	Chicago Bears	W 34-31
4	25-Sep-83	at Dallas Cowboys	L 21-20
5	2-Oct-83	Miami Dolphins	W 17-7
6	9-Oct-83	at Atlanta Falcons	W 19-17
7	16-Oct-83	San Francisco 49ers	L 32-13
8	23-Oct-83	at Tampa Bay Buccaneers	W 24-21
9	30-Oct-83	at Buffalo Bills	L 27-21
10	6-Nov-83	Atlanta Falcons	W 27-10
11	13-Nov-83	at San Francisco 49ers	L 27-0
12	21-Nov-83	New York Jets	L 31-28
13	27-Nov-83	Minnesota Vikings	W 17-16
14	4-Dec-83	at New England Patriots	L 7-0
15	11-Dec-83	at Philadelphia Eagles	W 20-17
16	18-Dec-83	Los Angeles Rams	L 26-24

1984 – 18ᵀᴴ SEASON

While the 7-9 record was a slight step backward from 1983, the Saints did have some good moments in 1984. They won their first Monday Night Football game, and until the last few games, the Saints were playoff hopefuls. Unfortunately, they lost 3 of their last 4 games.

With 94 points, Morten Andersen was the Saints' leader in scoring, and with 12 sacks, Rickey Jackson led the defensive team.

The New Orleans Saints Story 24

John Mecom, Saints owner, put the team up for sale for the price of $75,000,000.

1984

Week	Date	Opponent	Score
1	2-Sep-84	Atlanta Falcons	L 36-28
2	9-Sep-84	Tampa Bay Buccaneers	W 17-13
3	16-Sep-84	at San Francisco 49ers	L 30-20
4	23-Sep-84	St. Louis Cardinals	W 34-24
5	30-Sep-84	at Houston Oilers	W 27-10
6	7-Oct-84	at Chicago Bears	L 20-7
7	14-Oct-84	Los Angeles Rams	L 28-10
8	21-Oct-84	at Dallas Cowboys	L 30-27
9	28-Oct-84	at Cleveland Browns	W 16-14
10	4-Nov-84	Green Bay Packers	L 23-13
11	11-Nov-84	at Atlanta Falcons	W 17-13
12	19-Nov-84	Pittsburgh Steelers	W 27-24
13	25-Nov-84	San Francisco 49ers	L 35-3
14	2-Dec-84	at Los Angeles Rams	L 34-21
15	9-Dec-84	Cincinnati Bengals	L 24-21
16	15-Dec-84	at New York Giants	W 10-3

1985 – 19TH SEASON

The 1985 season was another heartbreak for Saints fans with a huge step in the wrong direction for the team, stumbling to a 5-11 record. The awful season led to Bum Phillips's resignation after week 12. Bum's son, Wade Phillips, took over for the rest of the season.

On May 21, 1985, local businessman, bank investor, and car dealership owner, Tom Benson purchases the Saints from

History 25

John Mecom, preventing a rumored purchase by other investors that would have moved the Saints to Jacksonville, FL.

Running back George Rodgers was traded to Washington before the start of the season, allowing Earl Campbell more play. Unfortunately, Campbell only scored 1 touchdown during the entire season and rushed for 643 yards. Wayne Wilson was the team's leading rusher with 645 yards on 169 carries.

Quarterback Dave Wilson had 145 completions on 293 passes (49.48% completion ratio) for 1,843 yards with 11 touchdowns.

Backup quarterback Bobby Hebert put up better numbers with a 53.6% average of 97 completions on 181 attempts for 5 touchdowns and 4 interceptions.

A highlight for fans was kicker Morten Andersen's 89% field goal completion on 31 of 35 attempts for 120 points total on the year.

1985

Week	Date	Opponent	Score
1	8-Sep-85	Kansas City Chiefs	L 47-27
2	15-Sep-85	at Denver Broncos	L 34-23
3	22-Sep-85	Tampa Bay Buccaneers	W 20-13
4	29-Sep-85	at San Francisco 49ers	W 20-17
5	6-Oct-85	Philadelphia Eagles	W 23-21
6	13-Oct-85	at Los Angeles Raiders	L 23-13
7	20-Oct-85	at Atlanta Falcons	L 31-24
8	27-Oct-85	New York Giants	L 21-13
9	3-Nov-85	at Los Angeles Rams	L 28-10
10	10-Nov-85	Seattle Seahawks	L 27-3
11	17-Nov-85	at Green Bay Packers	L 38-14
12	24-Nov-85	at Minnesota Vikings	W 30-23
13	1-Dec-85	Los Angeles Rams	W 29-3
14	8-Dec-85	at St. Louis Cardinals	L 28-16
15	15-Dec-85	San Francisco 49ers	L 31-19
16	22-Dec-85	Atlanta Falcons	L 16-10

1986 – 20ᵀᴴ Season

1986 marks the start of new head coach Jim Mora's years with the Saints. Coming off the 5-11 season of 1985, it was a slight relief for fans to see the team improve to 7-9 in Jim Mora's first year.

1986 also marks the beginning of legendary general manager Jim Finks's tenure with the franchise.

Second and third draft picks were used acquire two running backs, Rueben Mayes, and Dalton Hilliard, a local LSU athlete. Pat Swilling, star linebacker, was also picked up in this year's draft.

The Saints started out with 1-3 record, but things picked up as the season progressed. Some highlights were Mel Gray's team record kick return of 101 yards. Rueben Mayes became the NFL Rookie of the Year, racking up 1,353 yards. Mayes was also selected to be in this year's Pro Bowl along with teammates Rickey Jackson and Morten Andersen.

Quarterback Dave Wilson retains his starting position, fending off local favorite Bobby Hebert.

1986

Week	Date	Opponent	Score
1	7-Sep-86	Atlanta Falcons	L 31-10
2	14-Sep-86	Green Bay Packers	W 24-10
3	21-Sep-86	at San Francisco 49ers	L 26-17
4	28-Sep-86	at New York Giants	L 20-17
5	5-Oct-86	Washington Redskins	L 14-6
6	12-Oct-86	at Indianapolis Colts	W 17-14
7	19-Oct-86	Tampa Bay Buccaneers	W 38-7
8	26-Oct-86	at New York Jets	L 28-23
9	2-Nov-86	San Francisco 49ers	W 23-10
10	9-Nov-86	Los Angeles Rams	W 6-0

11	16-Nov-86	at St. Louis Cardinals	W 16-7
12	23-Nov-86	at Los Angeles Rams	L 26-13
13	30-Nov-86	New England Patriots	L 21-20
14	7-Dec-86	Miami Dolphins	L 31-27
15	14-Dec-86	at Atlanta Falcons	W 14-9
16	21-Dec-86	at Minnesota Vikings	L 33-17

1987 – 21ST SEASON

12-3! The first winning season! The first playoff birth!

After 20 long seasons, the Saints finally give their fans a winning season and a taste of the playoffs, including a 9-game winning streak going into the playoffs.

In Week 6 of the season, after losing a close game to the 49ers, Coach Mora had this to say, "The Saints ain't good enough. We're close, and close don't mean shit. I'm tired of coming close. I'm pissed off right now. You bet your ass I am. I'm sick of coulda, woulda, shoulda, coming close, if only."
(http://en.wikipedia.org/wiki/Jim_E._Mora)

Rueben Mayes had a great year rushing for 917 yards on 243 carries, averaging 3.77 yards per carry, and running in 5 touchdowns.

Bobby Hebert "The Cajun Canon" was the starting quarterback and threw for 2,119 yards on 164 completions of 294 attempts for a 55.78% completion ratio and 15 touchdowns.

Morten Andersen led the entire league in scoring with 121 points, hitting a perfect 37 of 37 extra points and 28 of 36 field goals.

Mel Gray led the NFL with 352 yards on 24 punt returns, with a 14.66 average return.

The Saints defense was rated 4th in the league, and #1 in interceptions with 30. Pat Swilling had 10.5 sacks, and Rickey Jackson had 9.5.

Pro Bowl players were Dave Waymer and Sam Mills.

The New Orleans Saints Story 28

The playoffs weren't pretty for the Saints, being routed 44-10 by the Minnesota Vikings at home in the Super Dome. The Vikings had 4 turnovers, 2 sacks, and kept the Saints' offense limited to 149 yards.

The Saints finished 2nd in the NFC West to a Joe Montana-led 49ers.

1987

Week	Date	Opponent	Score
1	13-Sep-87	Cleveland Browns	W 28-21
2	20-Sep-87	at Philadelphia Eagles	L 27-21
3	4-Oct-87	Los Angeles Rams	W 37-10
4	11-Oct-87	at St. Louis Cardinals	L 24-19
5	18-Oct-87	at Chicago Bears	W 19-17
6	25-Oct-87	San Francisco 49ers	L 24-22
7	1-Nov-87	at Atlanta Falcons	W 38-0
8	8-Nov-87	at Los Angeles Rams	W 31-14
9	15-Nov-87	at San Francisco 49ers	W 26-24
10	22-Nov-87	New York Giants	W 23-14
11	29-Nov-87	at Pittsburgh Steelers	W 20-16
12	6-Dec-87	Tampa Bay Buccaneers	W 44-34
13	13-Dec-87	Houston Oilers	W 24-10
14	20-Dec-87	at Cincinnati Bengals	W 41-24
15	27-Dec-87	Green Bay Packers	W 33-24
PLAYOFFS			
Week	Date	Opponent	Score
1	3-Jan-88	Minnesota Vikings	L 44-10

1988 – 22ND SEASON

History 29

1988 was a good year for the Saints with a 10-6 record, the second winning season in a row. The draft yielded fan-favorite, Craig "Ironhead" Heyward.

The season opener was a game worthy of the Super Bowl with Bobby Hebert and the Saints versus Joe Montana and the 49ers. Despite leading 17-10 at the half and Bobby Hebert passing for 4 touchdowns in the game, the 49ers edged out the Saints 34-33. It is key to keep in mind that this 49ers team went on to win this year's Super Bowl.

The Saints beat the Dallas Cowboys on Monday Night Football, which was only the Saints' 2nd win in 8 appearances. Despite the first game loss to the 49ers, the Saints win 7 straight to a 7-1 record.

The Saints shut out the Denver Broncos 42-0, winning by the largest margin in Saints history. In the game, Mel Gray ran a punt return back 66 yards for a touchdown. Bobby Hebert was 20 of 23 passes for 194 yards, and 3 touchdowns with no interceptions. This performance earned Hebert NFC Player of the Week.

The Saints lost a few games toward the end of the season, including a blowout to the Vikings 45-3, but found themselves in a 3-way tie for the divisional title with San Francisco and Los Angeles. However, the tiebreaker rules did not play out in the Saints' favor, leaving them at home while the other 2 teams entered the playoffs.

Bobby Hebert had 280 completions on 478 passes (58.57% completion ratio) for 3,156 yards and 20 touchdowns.

On the ground, Dalton Hilliard was the team's rushing leader with 823 yards (4.03 yards per carry) on 204 carries for 5 touchdowns.

Eric Martin racked up 1,083 yards on 85 catches.

Sam Mills, Eric Martin, and Morten Andersen all went to the Pro Bowl.

1988

Week	Date	Opponent	Score
1	4-Sep-88	San Francisco 49ers	L 34-33
2	11-Sep-88	at Atlanta Falcons	W 29-21

The New Orleans Saints Story 30

3	18-Sep-88	at Detroit Lions	W 22-14
4	25-Sep-88	Tampa Bay Buccaneers	W 13-9
5	3-Oct-88	Dallas Cowboys	W 20-17
6	9-Oct-88	at San Diego Chargers	W 23-17
7	16-Oct-88	at Seattle Seahawks	W 20-19
8	23-Oct-88	Los Angeles Raiders	W 20-6
9	30-Oct-88	Los Angeles Rams	L 12-10
10	6-Nov-88	at Washington Redskins	L 27-24
11	13-Nov-88	at Los Angeles Rams	W 14-10
12	20-Nov-88	Denver Broncos	W 42-0
13	27-Nov-88	New York Giants	L 13-12
14	4-Dec-88	at Minnesota Vikings	L 45-3
15	11-Dec-88	at San Francisco 49ers	L 30-17
16	18-Dec-88	Atlanta Falcons	W 10-9

1989 – 23RD SEASON

In the draft, the Saints pick up Wayne Martin who would start the next year and play with the Saints until 1999, handing out 82.5 sacks during his tenure in New Orleans.

The first game was a blow out of the Dallas Cowboys, 28-0. Bobby Hebert had a great day going 16 for 19 passes. Dallas was kept to a meager 20 yards rushing and 174 total offensive yards.

Inexplicably, the Saints would falter and lose the next 4 games. Even more bizarre and disheartening was star linebacker Rickey Jackson getting injured in a motorcycle accident. Following the accident, it was expected for Rickey to miss the next 4-6 weeks. Jackson had surgery on his fractured cheekbone and returned to play after missing only 2 games. He used a special facemask and had his jaw wired shut. Despite playing while recovering from his accident, he managed to get 2 sacks

History 31

against the Jets. An unfortunate aspect of the injury was it broke Jackson's team record of starting in consecutive games. Fortunately for the team, Jackson didn't let the injury stop him from having a great year.

The Saints found themselves at 6-7 and out of the playoff race, so Bobby Hebert was benched allowing backup quarterback John Fourcade to have an opportunity to play. Surprisingly Fourcade put up amazing numbers and won the remaining 3 games, passing for 302 yards versus the Bills, throwing 3 touchdowns versus the Eagles, and passing for 291 yards and 2 touchdowns versus the Colts.

Bobby Hebert finished the year with 2,686 yards with a 58.6 completion ratio, 20 touchdowns, and 15 interceptions.

Eric Martin was the leading receiver with 1,090 yards on 68 receptions.

Datlon Hilliard racked up 1,262 rushing yards, putting him 3rd in the NFC, and he had 13 rushing touchdowns and 5 receiving touchdowns.

On defense, Pat Swilling had an astounding 16.5 sacks, followed by Frank Warren with 9.5 sacks, and Rickey Jackson with 7.5 sacks.

Pro Bowlers were Dalton Hilliard, Pat Swilling, and Vaughn Johnson.

1989

Week	Date	Opponent	Score
1	10-Sep-89	Dallas Cowboys	W 28-0
2	17-Sep-89	at Green Bay Packers	L 35-34
3	24-Sep-89	at Tampa Bay Buccaneers	L 20-10
4	1-Oct-89	Washington Redskins	L 16-14
5	8-Oct-89	San Francisco 49ers	L 24-20
6	15-Oct-89	New York Jets	W 29-14
7	22-Oct-89	at Los Angeles Rams	W 40-21
8	29-Oct-89	Atlanta Falcons	W 20-13
9	6-Nov-89	at San Francisco 49ers	L 31-13
10	12-Nov-89	at New England	W 28-24

The New Orleans Saints Story 32

		Patriots	
11	19-Nov-89	at Atlanta Falcons	W 26-17
12	26-Nov-89	Los Angeles Rams	L 20-17
13	3-Dec-89	at Detroit Lions	L 21-14
14	10-Dec-89	at Buffalo Bills	W 22-19
15	18-Dec-89	Philadelphia Eagles	W 30-20
16	24-Dec-89	Indianapolis Colts	W 41-6

1990 – 24th Season

An 8-8 season with a playoff birth turned out to be somewhat of a mixed bag for Saints' fans. It was the Saints' worst record and first non-winning season in 3 years, yet they made the playoffs. It is a sad anomaly in the NFL that a team can play much worse than the year before and make it to the playoffs on the weaker performance where the better one was unrewarded.

Renaldo Turnbull and Vince Buck were picked in the first round of this year's draft. Turnbull had 44.5 sacks over his 6-year stay with the Saints, contributing to their legendary defense.

Fitting for the team, a Morten Andersen field goal in the final 2 seconds of the last game of the season was the clincher to place the Saints in the playoffs. Unfortunately, the Saints lost the first playoff game to the Chicago Bears by a score of 16-6.

The big story of the season was Bobby Hebert sitting out a year due to a contract dispute with the Saints. Quarterbacks Steve Walsh and John Fourcade split the season, but could not produce Hebert's numbers. Fourcade had a 43.1 completion percentage (compare to his 57% in the 3 games from the prior year), and Walsh had a 53.5. Bobby Hebert's completion percentage from the previous year was a 62.9 and the next year turned out to be a 60.1. Arguably, the Saints missed out on what could have been Hebert's most productive season, and many Saints' fans pine over what might have been if Hebert were taking the snaps in this year's playoffs. This is considered by some fans to be Jim Finks' only mistake in his long service to the Saints.

1990

Week	Date	Opponent	Score
1	10-Sep-90	San Francisco 49ers	L 13-12
2	16-Sep-90	at Minnesota Vikings	L 32-3
3	23-Sep-90	Phoenix Cardinals	W 28-7
4	Bye		
5	7-Oct-90	at Atlanta Falcons	L 28-27
6	14-Oct-90	Cleveland Browns	W 25-20
7	21-Oct-90	at Houston Oilers	L 23-10
8	28-Oct-90	Detroit Lions	L 27-10
9	4-Nov-90	at Cincinnati Bengals	W 21-7
10	11-Nov-90	Tampa Bay Buccaneers	W 35-7
11	18-Nov-90	at Washington Redskins	L 31-17
12	25-Nov-90	Atlanta Falcons	W 10-7
13	2-Dec-90	at Dallas Cowboys	L 17-13
14	9-Dec-90	at Los Angeles Rams	W 24-20
15	16-Dec-90	Pittsburgh Steelers	L 9-6
16	23-Dec-90	at San Francisco 49ers	W 13-10
17	31-Dec-90	Los Angeles Rams	W 20-17
PLAYOFFS			
Week	Date	Opponent	Score
Wildcard	6-Jan-91	at Chicago Bears	L 16-6

1991 – 25TH SEASON

The New Orleans Saints Story 34

The return of Bobby Hebert, an 11-5 Season, the first ever Divisional Championship, and a Return to the Playoffs—not a bad year for Saints' fans.

The Saints started off the year 7-0, the best start in franchise history. A big highlight was in Morten Andersen kicking a 60-yard field goal in a game against the Chicago Bears.

Floyd Turner was the new surprise on offense racking up 927 yards on only 64 catches with 8 touchdowns (14.48 yards per catch).

Quarterback duties were still split, but this year they were split between Bobby Hebert and Steve Walsh. Hebert's numbers were better as seen in the chart below, but the bigger factor was the Saints were 9-2 with Hebert calling the snaps and 2-3 with Walsh.

	Bobby Hebert	**Steve Walsh**
Completions	149	141
Total Passes	248	255
Completion %	60.1%	55.3%
Total Passing Yards	1,676	1,638
Touchdowns	9	11
Interceptions	8	6

Clearly, Hebert led in all categories except interceptions and touchdowns, including achieving 8 more completions and 38 more yards on 7 less pass attempts than Walsh. While Hebert was criticized for too harshly chastising his teammates on missed plays, the team certainly played better with him on the field.

A highlight of the season was the Saints defense, known and feared as "The Dome Patrol", being #1 in the league by allowing the fewest points. Pat Swilling led the league with 17 sacks and was voted Defensive Player of the Year.

For the 3rd time in the 6 years since Mora and Finks took over the Saints, the team went to the playoffs. Unfortunately, the Saints lost to rival Atlanta Falcons by a score of 27-20, which was the second-highest score the Saints defense had allowed all year.

1991

Week	Date	Opponent	Score
1	1-Sep-91	Seattle Seahawks	W 27-24
2	8-Sep-91	at Kansas City Chiefs	W 17-10
3	15-Sep-91	Los Angeles Rams	W 24-7
4	22-Sep-91	Minnesota Vikings	W 26-0
5	29-Sep-91	at Atlanta Falcons	W 27-6
6	Bye		
7	13-Oct-91	at Philadelphia Eagles	W 13-6
8	20-Oct-91	Tampa Bay Buccaneers	W 23-7
9	27-Oct-91	Chicago Bears	L 20-17
10	3-Nov-91	at Los Angeles Rams	W 24-17
11	10-Nov-91	San Francisco 49ers	W 10-3
12	17-Nov-91	at San Diego Chargers	L 24-21
13	24-Nov-91	Atlanta Falcons	L 23-20
14	1-Dec-91	at San Francisco 49ers	L 38-24
15	8-Dec-91	at Dallas Cowboys	L 23-14
16	16-Dec-91	Los Angeles Raiders	W 27-0
17	22-Dec-91	at Phoenix Cardinals	W 27-3
PLAYOFFS			
Week	Date	Opponent	Score
1	28-Dec-91	Atlanta Falcons	L 27-20

1992 – 26ᵀᴴ Season

12-4 and another trip to the playoffs. It was becoming a very consistent story for Saints's fans—a fun ride that ends badly.

Pro Bowlers were the entire "Dome Patrol" of Pat Swilling, Rickey Jackson, Sam Mills, and Vaughn Johnson, proving that the Saints' defense was not only good, but legendary, and arguably the best the NFL has ever seen.

The New Orleans Saints Story 36

Bobby Hebert was back at being the starter and was definitely "The Cajun Canon" with the stats he put up. He completed 249 passes on 422 attempts for a 59% completion ratio to attain 3,287 yards and 19 touchdowns.

In the air, Eric Martin led the team again with 1,041 yards on 68 receptions for a 15.31–yard average and 5 touchdowns. On the ground, Vaughn Dunbar was the team's leading rusher with 565 yards.

Morten Andersen had 120 points, was 29 of 34 in field goal attempts, and made 33 of 34 in extra points.

The Saints were in their 4th playoff game versus the Philadelphia Eagles in front of a home crowd in the Superdome. The Saints were up 20-7 late in the 3rd quarter. The Saints truly unraveled after that, giving up 2 interceptions and a safety on offense, and 2 touchdowns on defense.

Was it frustrating to see the Saints go 0-4 in the playoffs? Sure. But, it was a heck of a lot better than anything that came before 1986, Jim Mora, and Jim Finks.

Sadly, this would be the last season that Bobby Hebert and Pat Swilling would wear a Saints' uniform, and it would also mark the last Saints playoff appearance for 8 more years.

1992

Week	Date	Opponent	Score
1	6-Sep-92	at Philadelphia Eagles	L 15-13
2	13-Sep-92	Chicago Bears	W 28-6
3	20-Sep-92	at Atlanta Falcons	W 10-7
4	27-Sep-92	San Francisco 49ers	L 16-10
5	4-Oct-92	at Detroit Lions	W 13-7
6	11-Oct-92	Los Angeles Rams	W 13-10
7	18-Oct-92	at Phoenix Cardinals	W 30-21
8	Bye		
9	1-Nov-92	Tampa Bay Buccaneers	W 23-21
10	8-Nov-92	at New England Patriots	W 31-14
11	15-Nov-92	at San Francisco 49ers	L 21-20
12	23-Nov-92	Washington Redskins	W 20-3

History 37

13	29-Nov-92	Miami Dolphins	W 24-13
14	3-Dec-92	Atlanta Falcons	W 22-14
15	13-Dec-92	at Los Angeles Rams	W 37-14
16	20-Dec-92	Buffalo Bills	L 20-16
17	26-Dec-92	at New York Jets	W 20-0
PLAYOFFS			
Week	Date	Opponent	Score
1	3-Jan-93	Philadelphia Eagles	L 36-20

1993 – 27th Season

After the past 2 years of going 11-5 and 12-4, 8-8 was a certain disappointment in 1993.

Bobby Hebert was gone, now a quarterback for the rival Atlanta Falcons. On only the second game of the season, the two teams would face each other. On an interesting note, Bobby Hebert took over as starting quarterback in 1987 and remained so until 1992 skipping 1990 for a contract dispute. In his five years, the Saints went to the playoffs 3 times, and had 5 winning seasons, the only 5 winning Seasons the Saints would have until 2000. Just to emphasize the point, the only winning 5 seasons the Saints had before year 2000, came with Bobby Hebert taking the snaps. The only time the Saints did not have a winning season from 1987-1992 was in 1991 when Bobby was not playing.

Wade Wilson was brought in as a free agent and started off the season well by going 5-0. Sadly for the Saints, Wilson's performance diminished as the season went on, losing 8 of their last 11 games.

The draft brought in Willie Roaf in the first round as the eighth overall pick. Roaf, who was an offensive tackle from Louisiana Tech, would spend 9 years as a Saint and would become a 7-time Pro Bowl recipient. The cost of drafting Willie Roaf was trading standout linebacker Pat Swilling to the Detroit Lions for their first pick in the draft.

The New Orleans Saints Story 38

The Saints would face Bobby Hebert as a Falcon twice this season, going 1-1 against their rival. During the second week of the season the Saints met the Falcons in Atlanta. It was a hard-fought and close game. The Saints went into the 3rd quarter up 31-10. However, the 4th quarter was all Hebert's, throwing two touchdown passes, including a 98-yard reception to Michael Haynes, and getting his team within range for a field goal, tying the score at 31. In true Saints' fashion of the time, Morten Andersen won the game with a 44-yard field goal, making the final score 34-31.

Homecoming Rematch. 6 weeks later in the Superdome, Bobby Hebert plays his first game against the Saints in New Orleans. Fan reception to Bobby Hebert was one of appreciation and respect, but they also wanted their Saints to win. Thanks to 11 penalties, 2 turnovers, and being grossly outrushed by Atlanta, the Saints lost 15-25. It was a poor day for the New Orleans offense, having 8 of their 15 points result from 2 field goals and a safety.

No playoffs and no winning season.

Pro Bowl players were Tyrone Hughes, Rickey Jackson, and Renaldo Turnbull.

1993

Week	Date	Opponent	Score
1	5-Sep-93	Houston Oilers	W 33-21
2	12-Sep-93	at Atlanta Falcons	W 34-31
3	19-Sep-93	Detroit Lions	W 14-3
4	26-Sep-93	San Francisco 49ers	W 16-13
5	3-Oct-93	at Los Angeles Rams	W 37-6
6	Bye		
7	17-Oct-93	at Pittsburgh Steelers	L 37-14
8	24-Oct-93	Atlanta Falcons	L 26-15
9	31-Oct-93	at Phoenix Cardinals	W 20-17
10	Bye		
11	14-Nov-93	Green Bay Packers	L 19-17
12	22-Nov-93	at San Francisco 49ers	L 42-7
13	28-Nov-93	at Minnesota Vikings	W 17-14

History 39

14	5-Dec-93	at Cleveland Browns	L 17-13
15	12-Dec-93	Los Angeles Rams	L 23-20
16	20-Dec-93	New York Giants	L 24-14
17	26-Dec-93	at Philadelphia Eagles	L 37-26
18	2-Jan-94	Cincinnati Bengals	W 20-13

1994 – 28th Season

The Saints season record dropped from 1993's 8-8 to 7-9. This steady decline will continue until Jim Mora's eventual departure, and the Saints won't rebound for 2 head coaches after that.

Saints brought in Jim Everett as starting quarterback. Before Everett ever took the field as a Saint, he made headlines. Everett's past included being a record-breaking quarterback at Purdue, being a 1986 1st round draft pick, and playing with the Los Angeles Rams from 1986-1993. As a Ram, he brought his team to the playoffs in 1986, 1988, and 1989, including going to the 1989 NFC Championship Game. Back in 1985, Everett was ranked highest in total offense in the NCAA and setting a Purdue school record with 3,589 yards. Coincidentally, his Purdue record was eventually broken by future Saints quarterback, Drew Brees. In the NFL, Everett is ranked 14th All-Time in passing yards with 34,837 and 25th All-Time in touchdown passes with 203. He also made it to the Pro Bowl in 1991.

Strangely, these accomplishments were not what created the biggest stir upon Everett's arrival. During the 1989 NFC Championship Game against the 49ers, he was sacked repeatedly. Everett was so roughed up that at one point in the game he fell down in anticipation of another sack before anyone on the defense touched him. This has been called the "phantom sack," and detractors used it to claim that Everett's play suffered because he was afraid of taking a hit. One sports personality who used this to insult Everett was Jim Rome, who would refer to Jim Everett as Chris Everett, who was a female tennis player.

All this came to a head when Jim Everett was on Jim Rome's television show, *Talk2,* on *ESPN* in 1994. The exchange followed like this:

Rome (Host): "Jim, good to have you on the show."
Everett (Quarterback): "Good to be here, Jim. Thank you."
Rome: "Check that. Chris Everett, good to have you on the show."
Everett: "You know what? You know you've been calling me that for about the last five years."
Rome: "No, two years actually, Chris."
Everett: "Well, hey, you know what? Let me…let me say one thing. In that game how many sacks did we have that we came back and won?"
Rome: "How many sacks did you have?"
Everett: "Yeah, how many game—how many sacks?"
Rome: "But you see this was back in 1989. You may—you may have even been Jim Everett back there. But somewhere along the way, Jim, you ceased being Jim and you became Chris."
Everett: "Well, let me tell you a little secret. That, you know, we're sitting here right now, and if you guys want to take a station break you can, but if you call me Chris Everett to my face one more time."
Rome: "I already did it twice."
Everett: "You better—you better--call it one more time we better take a station break."
Rome: "Well, it's a five minute segment, a five segment show. We got a long way to go."
Everett: "We do."
Rome: "We got a long way to go."
Everett: "We do."
Rome: "I'll get a couple segments out of you before." (sic)
Everett: "Well, it's good to be here with you though."
Rome: "Well, it's good to see you too."
Everett: "You know, because you've been talking like this behind my back for a long time."
Rome: "But now I said it right here."
Everett: "Right. Exactly."

History 41

Rome: "Well, we got no problems then."
Everett: "I think it—I think that you probably won't say it again."
Rome: "I bet I do."
Everett: "Okay."
Rome: "Chris."

At this point, Jim Everett flipped the small, circular table between them over, and Everett's hands went to the chest area of Rome's sports jacket. Rome fell to the floor off the platform, and Everett stood straddled over him. Everett was certainly free to throw punches at this time, but did not. Someone, who seemed to work on the show, ran onto the screen and grabbed at Everett to pull him away from Rome who was still on the floor beneath him.

Jim Everett confronting Jim Rome on the air certainly got the attention of New Orleans as well as the sporting world. But, the real issue was whether Everett would deliver as quarterback, as some critics thought Everett's best years were behind him.

The 1994 season proved to be a good one for Everett, actually a much better year for him than the Saints. Everett's 3,855 yards was a Saints team record that stood until 2006 when it was beaten by Drew Brees. With 346 completions on 540 attempts, Everett produced a 64.1 completion percentage (the highest in his NFL career) and 22 touchdowns with 18 interceptions.

In the air, Quinn Early had the most receptions with 82 grabs for 894 yards with 4 touchdowns. With less receptions but more yards and touchdowns, Michael Hayes caught for 985 yards on 77 catches with 5 touchdowns.

On the ground, Mario Bates in his rookie year had the most rushing yards with 579 and 7 touchdowns.

Morten Andersen kicked for 116 points.

Pro Bowl players were Wayne Martin and Willie Roaf.

1994

Week	Date	Opponent	Score
1	4-Sep-94	at Kansas City Chiefs	L 30-17
2	11-Sep-94	Washington Redskins	L 38-24
3	18-Sep-94	at Tampa Bay	W 9-7

The New Orleans Saints Story 42

		Buccaneers	
4	25-Sep-94	at San Francisco 49ers	L 24-13
5	2-Oct-94	New York Giants	W 27-22
6	9-Oct-94	at Chicago Bears	L 17-7
7	16-Oct-94	San Diego Chargers	L 36-22
8	23-Oct-94	Los Angeles Rams	W 37-34
9	Bye		
10	6-Nov-94	at Minnesota Vikings	L 21-20
11	13-Nov-94	Atlanta Falcons	W 33-32
12	20-Nov-94	at Los Angeles Raiders	L 24-19
13	28-Nov-94	San Francisco 49ers	L 35-14
14	4-Dec-94	at Los Angeles Rams	W 31-15
15	11-Dec-94	at Atlanta Falcons	W 29-20
16	19-Dec-94	Dallas Cowboys	L 24-16
17	24-Dec-94	at Denver Broncos	W 30-28

1995 – 29th Season

Another 7-9 year. Another good year from Jim Everett. No real improvement.

The Saints lost the first 5 games of the season, but won 7 of the last 11.

Everett passed for 3,970 yards on 345 completions of 567 passes for 60.8 completion ratio. He had 26 touchdowns, his best since 1989, with 14 interceptions. In short, less interceptions, more touchdowns, more yards, but a slightly lower completion percentage.

Mario Bates was the leading rusher again with 954 yards and 244 attempts with a 3.91 yard per carry average. Leading receiver was Quinn Early with 1,087 yards on 81 grabs for a 13.42 average reception with 8 touchdowns.

This season was the first without Morten Andersen who went to the rival Atlanta Falcons, where Bobby Hebert and Craig

History 43

"Ironhead" Heyward were also on the roster. Andersen put up 122 points this year for the Falcons, while his replacements with the Saints, Doug Brien and Chip Lomiller, kicked for 128 points combined. However, neither Brien or Lomiller could compare to Andersen's accuracy. Brien made 19 of 29 field goals attempts for 66% accuracy, and Lomiller made 8 of 14 field goal attempts for 57%. Andersen nailed 31 of 37 field goals for an 83.8%.

1995

Week	Date	Opponent	Score
1	3-Sep-95	San Francisco 49ers	L 24-22
2	10-Sep-95	at St. Louis Rams	L 17-13
3	17-Sep-95	Atlanta Falcons	L 27-24
4	24-Sep-95	at New York Giants	L 45-29
5	1-Oct-95	Philadelphia Eagles	L 15-10
6	Bye		
7	15-Oct-95	Miami Dolphins	W 33-30
8	22-Oct-95	at Carolina Panthers	L 20-3
9	29-Oct-95	at San Francisco 49ers	W 11-7
10	5-Nov-95	St. Louis Rams	W 19-10
11	12-Nov-95	Indianapolis Colts	W 17-14
12	19-Nov-95	at Minnesota Vikings	L 43-24
13	26-Nov-95	Carolina Panthers	W 34-26
14	3-Dec-95	at New England Patriots	W 31-17
15	10-Dec-95	at Atlanta Falcons	L 19-14
16	16-Dec-95	Green Bay Packers	L 34-23
17	24-Dec-95	at New York Jets	W 12-0

1996 – 30TH SEASON

The New Orleans Saints Story 44

The Saints 30th Season was an utter disaster. There were very little of the elements remaining that had made the Saints so successful during Coach Mora's initial run with team. Bobby Hebert was gone, Pat Swilling was gone, Hiliard and Mayes were long gone, and Morten Andersen was still kicking amazingly well with the Atlanta Falcons. Andersen was a key component to a primarily defensive team. The Saints had one of the best defenses the NFL had ever seen, but did not have explosive wide receivers such as Jerry Rice. Getting points every time the team got within field goal range was considered guaranteed, often taken for granted, points with Morten Andersen, and that worked well with the Saints and Mora's conservative coaching style. Playing conservative offensive football without a solid kicker and an all-around strong defense is a recipe for disaster. In this case, it cooked up a 3-13 season, the worst seen in New Orleans since 1980.

After losing to the Carolina Panthers to bring the Saints' record to 2-6, Jim Mora had this to say, "Well, what happened was, that second game, we got our ass kicked. In the second half, we just got our ass totally kicked. We couldn't do diddly poo offensively, we couldn't make a first down, we couldn't run the ball, we didn't try to run the ball, we couldn't complete a pass - we sucked. The second half, we sucked. We couldn't stop the run. Every time they got the ball, they went down and got points. We got our ass totally kicked in the second half - that's what it boiled down to. It was a horseshit performance in the second half. Horseshit. I'm totally embarrassed and totally ashamed. Coaching did a horrible job. The players did a horrible job. We got our ass kicked in that second half. It sucked. It stunk."

Many people think the above tirade included Mora's famous quote about "Playoffs!," but that happened several years later while he was coaching the Indianapolis Colts.

Mora resigned the next day bringing to an end the best era that the New Orleans Saints had ever experienced.

The Saints finished the season 3-13 under interim head coach Rick Venturi.

Jim Everett, who had two great seasons with the Saints, had a poorer showing in 1996 with only 2,797 yards passing and a 57.5% completion ratio. Those numbers certainly weren't bad, especially for a QB of a 3-13 team, but they were lower than his previous stats with the Saints. Everett would be a San Diego Charger the following year, leaving the Saints with a topsy-turvy struggle to find a suitable quarterback.

1996

Week	Date	Opponent	Score
1	1-Sep-96	at San Francisco 49ers	L 27-11
2	8-Sep-96	Carolina Panthers	L 22-20
3	15-Sep-96	at Cincinnati Bengals	L 30-15
4	22-Sep-96	Arizona Cardinals	L 28-14
5	29-Sep-96	at Baltimore Ravens	L 17-10
6	6-Oct-96	Jacksonville Jaguars	W 17-13
7	13-Oct-96	Chicago Bears	W 27-24
8	20-Oct-96	at Carolina Panthers	L 19-7
9	Bye		
10	3-Nov-96	San Francisco 49ers	L 24-17
11	10-Nov-96	Houston Oilers	L 31-14
12	17-Nov-96	at Atlanta Falcons	L 17-15
13	24-Nov-96	at Tampa Bay Buccaneers	L 13-7
14	1-Dec-96	St. Louis Rams	L 26-10
15	8-Dec-96	Atlanta Falcons	L 31-15
16	15-Dec-96	at New York Giants	W 17-3
17	21-Dec-96	at St. Louis Rams	L 14-13

1997 – 31ST SEASON

Interim coach Rick Venturi was replaced by Mike Ditka with a lot of hype and high expectations.

Ditka was famous for his coaching run with the Chicago Bears, which is especially remembered by New Orleanians since

The New Orleans Saints Story 46

the Bears won Super Bowl XX in the Super Dome in New Orleans on January 26, 1986. Detractors would claim that Ditka's success in Chicago had more to do with the scouting/drafting/trading work of Jim Finks that built a tremendously talented team and the football expertise of his assistant coaching staff, especially defensive coordinator, Buddy Ryan. There seems to be some merit in the criticism as Finks built powerful defenses in each team that he worked for, and the 1985 Bears had the #1 defense in the NFL allowing only 4,135 yards and 198 points all season.

Before coaching, Ditka was a tight end and punter for the University of Pittsburgh. Ditka played in the NFL for the Chicago Bears, the Philadelphia Eagles, and the Dallas Cowboys. He was a first round draft pick in 1961, gained 5,812 yards on 427 receptions in his career, and was inducted into the Pro Football Hall of Fame in 1988.

Ditka refers to his time with the Saints as 3 of the worst years of his life. They were certainly 3 of the worst years of Saints football. Ditka's most criticized football decision was trading away all of the Saints' 1999 draft picks plus their 1st and 3rd round picks in 2000 in order to obtain Ricky Williams, a standout running back from the University of Texas, a Heisman Trophy winner and 2-time All-American. Williams set NCAA career records in rushing yards, touchdowns, and various other offense categories.

Williams certainly had remarkable talent, but no coach had ever bargained so much for one player, which made it a highly controversial move before Williams ever took the field. Ditka and Williams appeared on the cover for *ESPN The Magazine* in a mock wedding photo with Ditka dressed as the groom and Williams as the bride.

The 1997 Season itself saw 4 quarterbacks vying for the starting position without any of them being significantly better than another.

	%	Passes Attempted	Passes Completed	Passing Yards	TDs	Int
Heath Shuler	52.2%	203	106	1,288	2	14

History 47

Billy Joe Hobert	48.4%	161	79	1,024	6	10
Danny Wuerffel	46.2%	91	42	518	4	8
Doug Nussmeier	56.3%	32	18	183	0	3

All of the 4 quarterbacks threw more interceptions than touchdowns, and they all ranged between a 46-53% completion ratio. It's not hard to see why the team went only 6-10.

One of the few highlights of the 1997 Season was the kicking game. Doug Brien provided a solid season hitting 23 of 27 field goal attempts for an 85.19% and scoring 91 points. As means of comparison Morten Andersen produced the same numbers for Atlanta on 23 of 27 field goal attempts.

The only other positive mark for the Saints was the play of the defense, who recorded a team record of 58 sacks and were ranked 4th in total defense.

1997

Week	Date	Opponent	Score
1	31-Aug-97	at St. Louis Rams	L 38-24
2	7-Sep-97	San Diego Chargers	L 20-6
3	14-Sep-97	at San Francisco 49ers	L 33-7
4	21-Sep-97	Detroit Lions	W 35-17
5	28-Sep-97	at New York Giants	L 14-9
6	5-Oct-97	at Chicago Bears	W 20-17
7	12-Oct-97	Atlanta Falcons	L 23-17
8	19-Oct-97	Carolina Panthers	L 13-0
9	26-Oct-97	San Francisco 49ers	L 23-0
10	Bye		
11	9-Nov-97	at Oakland Raiders	W 13-10
12	16-Nov-97	Seattle Seahawks	W 20-17
13	23-Nov-97	at Atlanta Falcons	L 20-3
14	30-Nov-97	at Carolina Panthers	W 16-13
15	7-Dec-97	St. Louis Rams	L 34-27

| 16 | 14-Dec-97 | Arizona Cardinals | W 27-10 |
| 17 | 21-Dec-97 | at Kansas City Chiefs | L 25-13 |

1998 – 32ND SEASON

Ditka year two. Another 6-10 showing.

The good: The Saints led the league in defensive touchdowns. Willie Roaf made the Pro Bowl. Kyle Turley started his first year with the Saints, and he was a personality on and off the field that sparked some interest from Saints fans without a lot else to be excited about. Kicker Doug Brien had another excellent year hitting 20 of 22 field goal attempts for a 90.9% field goal percentage.

The Bad: 1998 was another year of rotating quarterbacks, but this time it included 5 would-be snap-takers.

	%	Passes Attempted	Passes Completed	Passing Yards	TDs	Int
Kerry Collins	48.16%	353	170	2,213	12	15
Billy Joe Tollivar	55.56%	198	110	1,427	8	4
Danny Wuerffel	52.10%	119	62	695	5	5
Billy Joe Hobert	47.83%	23	11	170	1	0
Lamar Smith	50.00%	2	1	20	1	0

This year no quarterback would throw over a 55.56% completion ratio. It seems to be a ridiculous coaching decision to throw 5 different quarterbacks into regular season games. The common practice would be to pick a frontrunner in the preseason and give him time to mature and gain his footing by allowing him game time. If the starter struggles or is injured, then bring in the

History 49

backup or 2 different backups, and possibly give both of them consistent game time. The constant switching does not allow for one quarterback to get into a groove and become comfortable with his own abilities and familiar with the team in real-game situations. After all, Danny Wuerffel was a Heisman Trophy Winner in 1996 and was only allowed 119 passes with the Saints in 1998.

The Colts had a horrendous first year with Peyton Manning as quarterback, including the young Manning throwing 28 interceptions with fewer 26 touchdowns. However, the team invested game time in him and went from 3-13 in their first year to 13-3 in their second. Ditka didn't seem to have the ability to see the big picture and delay instant gratification in order to develop a quality quarterback. Admittedly, the Saints did not have a lot of offensive talent in 1998, but this quarterback coaching is questionable at any talent level.

In 1998, no rusher gained over 460 yards, and no receiver gained over 825 yards.

1998

Week	Date	Opponent	Score
1	6-Sep-98	at St. Louis Rams	W 24-17
2	13-Sep-98	Carolina Panthers	W 19-14
3	Bye		
4	27-Sep-98	at Indianapolis Colts	W 19-13
5	4-Oct-98	New England Patriots	L 30-27
6	11-Oct-98	San Francisco 49ers	L 31-0
7	18-Oct-98	at Atlanta Falcons	L 31-23
8	25-Oct-98	Tampa Bay Buccaneers	W 9-3
9	1-Nov-98	at Carolina Panthers	L 31-17
10	8-Nov-98	at Minnesota Vikings	L 31-24
11	15-Nov-98	St. Louis Rams	W 24-3
12	22-Nov-98	at San Francisco 49ers	L 31-20
13	29-Nov-98	at Miami Dolphins	L 30-10
14	6-Dec-98	Dallas Cowboys	W 22-3
15	13-Dec-98	Atlanta Falcons	L 27-17

The New Orleans Saints Story 50

| 16 | 20-Dec-98 | at Arizona Cardinals | L 19-17 |
| 17 | 27-Dec-98 | Buffalo Bills | L 45-33 |

1999 – 33ᴿᴰ Season

Ditka year 3. A 3-13 season.

1999 was the season Coach Ditka made the controversial trade to bring in Ricky Williams. It was the first time that an NFL team only acquired 1 player total in the draft. So everyone was watching to see if it would pay off.

Critics of Ditka's unorthodox draft decision seemed justified when Ricky Williams was injured in the first game of the preseason as a Saint. Before stepping onto the field for 1 regular season game, Williams was injured. This seemed to prove the validity of the criticism in riskily putting all of New Orleans' eggs in one basket. All draft picks were used on 1 player. Under normal circumstances and in any other team's draft besides Ditka's this year, 1 injury brings down 1 player, not a year's worth of draft picks, merely 1 one them. It was a gamble that seemed highly unlikely to pay off after the 1st playoff game injury.

Ricky would suffer several injuries during the season, but he still managed to put up 884 yards on 253 carries for a 3.49 yards per carry average. Those numbers are definitely a disappointment based on Williams' talent and college numbers, but they are better than what many experts were predicting after his preseason injury.

The same 4-man, revolving-door circus was going on at quarterback, but with Jake Delhomme this time.

	%	Passes Attempted	Passes Completed	Passing Yards	TDs	Int
Billy Joe Tollivar	268	1390	51.90%	1,916	7	16

Billy Joe Hobert	159	850	53.50%	970	6	6
Jake Delhomme	76	420	55.30%	521	3	5
Danny Wuerffel	48	22	45.80%	191	0	3

Delhomme was only allowed 76 passes which didn't provide enough play for his talent to be utilized or even noticed by many. Delhomme was a local athlete from Breaux Bridge, Louisiana, and an ideal candidate for a Saints quarterback. He was barely utilized at all by the Saints in 1999, not at all in 2000 and 2001, and very briefly in 2002. He was traded to the Carolina Panthers in 2003 and went 10-5 with 3,219 passing yards and helped take them to the Super Bowl, all in his very first year away from the Saints. The Delhomme situation is one of many in which Saints fans will talk about one of their players by saying, "Yeah, he'll be great the second we let him go to another team."

During the season the Saints had a 7-game losing streak, with 5 of those games involving the Saints blowing a lead going into the 4th quarter. Those are stereotypical Saints' losses, building up the fans' hopes and breaking their hearts in the end, often in the last few moments.

The only 2 positive points of the year were Willie Roaf going to the Pro Bowl for the 6th year in a row and Dan Brien going 24 for 29 in field goal attempts with an 82.8% field goal percentage.

The year ended with owner Tom Benson putting an axe to a slew of the staff, including firing general manager Bill Kuharich, head coah Mike Ditka, the entire rest of the coaching staff except Rick Venturi (linebacker coach and interim head coach following Mora's departure), and vice president Terry O'Neil.

1999

Week	Date	Opponent	Score
1	12-Sep-99	Carolina Panthers	W 19-10
2	19-Sep-99	at San Francisco 49ers	L 28-21

The New Orleans Saints Story 52

3	Bye		
4	3-Oct-99	at Chicago Bears	L 14-10
5	10-Oct-99	Atlanta Falcons	L 20-17
6	17-Oct-99	Tennessee Titans	L 24-21
7	24-Oct-99	at New York Giants	L 31-3
8	31-Oct-99	Cleveland Browns	L 21-16
9	7-Nov-99	Tampa Bay Buccaneers	L 31-16
10	14-Nov-99	San Francisco 49ers	W 24-6
11	21-Nov-99	at Jacksonville Jaguars	L 41-23
12	28-Nov-99	at St. Louis Rams	L 43-12
13	5-Dec-99	at Atlanta Falcons	L 35-12
14	12-Dec-99	St. Louis Rams	L 30-14
15	19-Dec-99	at Baltimore Ravens	L 31-8
16	24-Dec-99	Dallas Cowboys	W 31-24
17	2-Jan-00	at Carolina Panthers	L 45-13

2000 – 34TH SEASON

Ditka was gone. The fans were excited to see a change. Fans were hopeful, but often skeptical. Surely, no one was anticipating a 10-6 season with a trip to the playoffs, including the Saints' first ever playoff win.

Randy Mueller was brought in as the new general manager. Jim Haslett was brought in by Tom Benson to be the new head coach.

The season started dismally with the typical "it's a rebuilding year" excuse from supporters and a 1-3 record. Then, the Saints went on a 6-game winning streak.

Starting quarterback Jeff Blake was having a great year until he broke his foot in the first loss vs. the Oakland Raiders following the 6-game winning streak. Blake was out for the year, bringing backup quarterback Aaron Brooks into the starting position.

Aaron Brooks fit in well with the offense that had been established earlier in the year. In fact his athletic playing style was quite similar to Jeff Blake. Brooks would go 3 wins-2 losses in the remaining 5 games of the regular season.

Ricky Williams had a better year with 1,000 rushing yards on 248 carries for a 4.03 yard per carry average and 8 touchdowns. Williams was injured in a game versus the Panthers and was out for the rest of the season. A poor reflection on the rest of the offense, 2 of the top 4 rushers were quarterbacks Jeff Blake with 243 yards (2nd highest on team) and Aaron Brooks with 170 yards (4th highest).

A popular and successful new addition to the team was Joe Horn, who caught 95 catches for 1,340 yards, which was a new team record, with a 14.10 yards per grab average and 8 touchdowns. Surprisingly, Ricky Williams caught 44 passes for 409 yards and 1 touchdown.

The postseason was the big news of the season, and came as a huge surprise after a 1-3 start, a new GM, a new VP, new coaches, new quarterbacks, a new receiver, and a star running back in his second year following a disappointing rookie season. Who would have guessed?

The Wild Card Game was held on December 30, 2000 in The Louisiana Super Dome. The Saints were playing against the defending Super Bowl champions, the St. Louis Rams. The Rams and the Saints had played each other twice during the regular season, the last game having taken place only 6 days earlier. They split victories in those 2 games, but the Rams had won the most recent contest.

The Saints beat the Rams 31-28 for their first playoff victory in franchise history. Aaron Brooks had an amazing game passing for 266 yards and 4 touchdowns. One of the telling stats from the game is Marshall Faulk, who ran for 220 yards versus the Saints earlier in the year, was held to a mere 24 rushing yards in this Wild Card game.

The second playoff game, the divisional playoffs, versus the Minnesota Vikings would not go so well for the Saints, losing 34-16. Vikings quarterback, Daunte Culpepper, threw for 305 yards and 3 touchdowns.

The New Orleans Saints Story 54

Pro Bowl recipients were Mark Fields, La'Roi Glover, Joe Johnson, Keith Mitchell, Willie Roaf, and Kyle Turley.

2000

Week	Date	Opponent	Score
1	3-Sep-00	Detroit Lions	L 14-10
2	10-Sep-00	at San Diego Chargers	W 28-27
3	17-Sep-00	at Seattle Seahawks	L 20-10
4	24-Sep-00	Philadelphia Eagles	L 21-7
5	Bye		
6	8-Oct-00	at Chicago Bears	W 31-10
7	15-Oct-00	Carolina Panthers	W 24-6
8	22-Oct-00	at Atlanta Falcons	W 21-19
9	29-Oct-00	at Arizona Cardinals	W 21-10
10	5-Nov-00	San Francisco 49ers	W 31-15
11	12-Nov-00	at Carolina Panthers	W 20-10
12	19-Nov-00	Oakland Raiders	L 31-22
13	26-Nov-00	at St. Louis Rams	W 31-24
14	3-Dec-00	Denver Broncos	L 38-23
15	10-Dec-00	at San Francisco 49ers	W 31-27
16	17-Dec-00	Atlanta Falcons	W 23-7
17	24-Dec-00	St. Louis Rams	L 26-21
PLAYOFFS			
Week	Date	Opponent	Score
Wildcard	30-Dec-00	St. Louis Rams	W 31-28
Division	6-Jan-01	at Minnesota Vikings	L 34-16

2001 – 35th Season

The Saints fall apart. Unfortunately, the Saints will never perform as well with Haslett as coach as they did in their first year.

History 55

Ricky Williams and Joe Horn had great years. Williams had 1,245 rushing yards on 313 carries for a 4.0 yards per carry average and 6 touchdowns. Williams also made 60 catches for 511 yards. Sadly, it would be Ricky's last year as a Saint. Joe Horn caught 83 passes for 1,265 yards for a 15.24 reception average and 9 touchdowns.

Willy Jackson, 2nd on the team in receptions, also had a great year with 81 catches for 1,046 yards for a 12.91 yards per reception average.

The Saints picked up Deuce McAllister in the draft. Although he only ran the ball 16 times, Deuce racked up 92 yards for a 5.75 yard per carry average.

New kicker, John Carney, made 27 of 31 field goal attempts for an 87.09% and 117 points.

Aaron Brooks' hit on 312 of 558 passes for a 55.9 completion ratio and 3,832 yards with 26 touchdowns and 22 interceptions.

Somehow with all these accomplishments, the Saints couldn't even pull off a winning season, much less another playoff run. The mistakes that were made came at very inopportune times, and that will keep any NFL team out of the post season.

2001

Week	Date	Opponent	Score
1	9-Sep-01	at Buffalo Bills	W 24-6
3	30-Sep-01	at New York Giants	L 21-13
4	7-Oct-01	Minnesota Vikings	W 28-15
5	14-Oct-01	at Carolina Panthers	W 27-25
6	21-Oct-01	Atlanta Falcons	L 20-13
7	28-Oct-01	at St. Louis Rams	W 34-31
8	4-Nov-01	New York Jets	L 16-9
9	11-Nov-01	at San Francisco 49ers	L 28-27
10	18-Nov-01	Indianapolis Colts	W 34-20
11	25-Nov-01	at New England Patriots	L 34-17
12	2-Dec-01	Carolina Panthers	W 27-23

13	9-Dec-01	at Atlanta Falcons	W 28-10
14	17-Dec-01	St. Louis Rams	L 34-21
15	23-Dec-01	at Tampa Bay Buccaneers	L 48-21
16	30-Dec-01	Washington Redskins	L 40-10
17	6-Jan-02	San Francisco 49ers	L 38-0

2002 – 36ᵀᴴ Season

The Saints manage to improve to a 9-7 winning season, but they don't make the playoffs. This year was yet another heartbreaker for Saints followers, with the Saints starting 6-2 and going a pathetic 3-5 in the second half of the season, taking themselves out of the playoffs. The Saints found themselves at 9-4 and only needing to win one of their remaining 3 games to enter the playoffs. To make things look even better they were playing the Minnesota Vikings, Cincinnati Bengals, and Carolina Panthers, who were all already eliminated from the postseason. The Saints lost all 3 games, including the game to the Bengals who were only 1-14 going into the game. It was a truly self-destructive and painful end to the season.

Ricky Williams was gone to the Miami Dolphins, and much to the chagrin of Saints' fans, he had a league-leading year with 1,853 yards rushing on 383 carries for a 4.8 yards per carry average. All 3 of those numbers were far greater than anything he produced while wearing a Saints' jersey. He also caught 47 passes for 363 yards. Williams became one more player to add to the "achieved greatness as soon as he left the Saints" list.

Fortunately, Deuce McAllister stepped up and filled the void with a fantastic season of his own, racking up 1,388 yards on 325 carries for an average of 4.3 yards per carry and an impressive 13 touchdowns. All 4 of those stats were also better than any that were made by Ricky Williams as a Saint. Deuce also went to the Pro Bowl this year.

Joe Horn caught 88 passes for 1,312 yards and 7 touchdowns.

Aaron Brooks made 283 completions on 528 attempts for a 53.6% completion rate with 27 touchdowns and 15 interceptions.

Jake Delhomme in his last year as a Saint, only threw 10 passes but made 8 completions for 113 yards and an 80% completion ratio.

The Saints drafted Donte Stallworth.

2002

Week	Date	Opponent	Score
1	8-Sep-02	at Tampa Bay Buccaneers	W 26-20
2	15-Sep-02	Green Bay Packers	W 35-20
3	22-Sep-02	at Chicago Bears	W 29-23
4	29-Sep-02	at Detroit Lions	L 26-21
5	6-Oct-02	Pittsburgh Steelers	W 32-29
6	13-Oct-02	at Washington Redskins	W 43-27
7	20-Oct-02	San Francisco 49ers	W 35-27
8	27-Oct-02	Atlanta Falcons	L 37-35
9	Bye		
10	10-Nov-02	at Carolina Panthers	W 34-24
11	17-Nov-02	at Atlanta Falcons	L 24-17
12	24-Nov-02	Cleveland Browns	L 24-15
13	1-Dec-02	Tampa Bay Buccaneers	W 23-20
14	8-Dec-02	at Baltimore Ravens	W 37-25
15	15-Dec-02	Minnesota Vikings	L 32-31
16	22-Dec-02	at Cincinnati Bengals	L 20-13
17	29-Dec-02	Carolina Panthers	L 10-6

2003 – 37th Season

The Saints drop back to an 8-8 record.

Deuce McAllister had a tremendous year with 1,641 rushing yards with 8 touchdowns on 351 carries for a 4.68 yards per carry average. Deuce also caught 69 passes for 516 yards.

Joe Horn had a good year with 973 yards on 78 catches and 10 touchdowns. However, this year involved the controversial "cell phone" touchdown reception after which Horn took a cell phone he had placed in the padding around the base of the field goal post, resulting in a $30,000 fine for the receiver and some negative press. In fairness to Aaron Brooks, it was a rocket of a pass that was right on target.

Kicker John Carney's year slipped somewhat to hitting 22 of 30 field goal attempts for a 73.33% and 102 points.

Brooks had a higher completion rate of 59.1 (a career best) and threw 24 touchdowns to only 8 interceptions.

Once again there were some impressive stats, but a lack of consistency and ill-timed mistakes kept the Saints from getting the job done.

2003

Week	Date	Opponent	Score
1	7-Sep-03	at Seattle Seahawks	L 27-10
2	14-Sep-03	Houston Texans	W 31-10
3	21-Sep-03	at Tennessee Titans	L 27-17
4	28-Sep-03	Indianapolis Colts	L 55-21
5	5-Oct-03	at Carolina Panthers	L 19-13
6	12-Oct-03	Chicago Bears	W 20-13
7	19-Oct-03	at Atlanta Falcons	W 45-17
8	26-Oct-03	Carolina Panthers	L 23-20
9	2-Nov-03	at Tampa Bay Buccaneers	W 17-14
10	Bye		
11	16-Nov-03	Atlanta Falcons	W 23-20

12	23-Nov-03	at Philadelphia Eagles	L 33-20
13	30-Nov-03	at Washington Redskins	W 24-20
14	7-Dec-03	Tampa Bay Buccaneers	L 14-7
15	14-Dec-03	New York Giants	W 45-7
16	21-Dec-03	at Jacksonville Jaguars	L 20-19
17	28-Dec-03	Dallas Cowboys	W 13-7

2004 – 38ᵀᴴ Sᴇᴀsᴏɴ

Yet another mediocre 8-8 season.

Deuce McAllister rushed for 1,074 yards on 269 carries for a 3.99 yards per carry average and 9 touchdowns. Telling of the rest of the offense was that the next highest rusher only had 244 yards, and the 3rd highest rusher was quarterback Aaron Brooks at 173 yards.

Joe Horn had another stellar year with 1,399 yards on 94 catches with 10 touchdowns. Donte Stallworth also put up 578 receiving yards.

Aaron Brooks hit 309 of 542 passes for 3,810 yards and a 57.01 completion ratio. He had 21 touchdowns and 16 interceptions (twice as many as the previous season). At about this time, fans were becoming enraged at Brooks smiling on the sidelines after throwing an interception or making a critical error. Whether it reflected a cavalier attitude or was a horrible miscommunication between quarterback and fans, it happened frequently and many fans were ready for a new quarterback who would be more consistent, especially in clutch situations. In the least, they wanted a QB who seemed concerned with winning and playing well.

John Carney picked his numbers up from the previous season to make 22 of 27 field goal attempts for an 81.48 FG% and 104 points.

The New Orleans Saints Story 60
2004

Week	Date	Opponent	Score
1	12-Sep-04	Seattle Seahawks	L 21-7
2	19-Sep-04	San Francisco 49ers	W 30-27
3	26-Sep-04	at St. Louis Rams	W 28-25
4	3-Oct-04	at Arizona Cardinals	L 34-10
5	10-Oct-04	Tampa Bay Buccaneers	L 20-17
6	17-Oct-04	Minnesota Vikings	L 38-31
7	24-Oct-04	at Oakland Raiders	W 31-26
8	Bye		
9	7-Nov-04	at San Diego Chargers	L 43-17
10	14-Nov-04	Kansas City Chiefs	W 27-20
11	21-Nov-04	Denver Broncos	L 34-13
12	28-Nov-04	at Atlanta Falcons	L 24-21
13	5-Dec-04	Carolina Panthers	L 32-21
14	12-Dec-04	at Dallas Cowboys	W 27-13
15	19-Dec-04	at Tampa Bay Buccaneers	W 21-17
16	26-Dec-04	Atlanta Falcons	W 26-13
17	2-Jan-05	at Carolina Panthers	W 21-18

2005 – 39TH SEASON

The 2005 season was marked by the unprecedented devastation caused to New Orleans and the Gulf coast area from Hurricane Katrina. The worst natural disaster in U.S. history made the New Orleans Saints the unofficial America's Team, and for one brief game, they were.

As residents from the area were scattered to surrounding states and trying to repair their property and lives, there were serious rumors about the New Orleans Saints being moved to San Antonio. San Antonio was where the Saints played several games in 2005 following Hurricane Katrina damaging the Super Dome and rendering it not suitable for play without millions of dollars in costly repair. What added scary validity to the rumor was team owner Tom Benson already owned car dealerships in San Antonio.

The opening game of the season for the Saints would take place on Septemeber 11, 2005, just 13 days after Hurricane Katrina hit on August 29th. The opponents were the Carolina Panthers. The Saints looked like a championship team in the season opener, and the entire country seemed to be rooting for them as they won 23-20. Unfortunately for New Orleans, it was not a game predicting the rest of the season as the Saints would stumble nearly all year to a 3-13 finish, while the defeated Panthers would go 11-5, finishing 1st in the NFC South and going all the way to the Conference Championship. In fact, the Saints' 3-13 record was the 2nd worst in all of the NFL.

Brooks had a terrible year with 17 interceptions to only 13 touchdowns. He has a 55.7 completion ratio with 2,882 yards. Brooks was benched for the last 3 games of the season and would never again take a snap as a Saint. Brooks was replaced with backup quarterback Todd Bouman whose 2005 stats would prove to be slightly worse than those of Brooks.

Deuce McAllister was injured fairly early in the season in October, leaving him with a torn ACL in his right knee. His performance this year was greatly limited by this injury. McAllister put up 335 yards on 93 carries for an average of 3.60 yards per carry.

Joe Horn had an off-year due to a hamstring injury. He made 49 catches for 654 yards and 1 touchdown. He was second in receiving to Donte Stallworth who stepped up to make 70 grabs for 945 yards and 7 touchdowns.

John Carney didn't have one of his better years as he made 25 of 32 field goal attempts for a 78.13 FG% and 97 points.

This year would be the last for coach Jim Haslett and Aaron Brooks.

One might speculate that there was some resentment left toward the Saints for not living up to their first game's potential and becoming the America's Team dream-story that the media so wanted them to be—rising out of the destruction of Katrina and dominating the NFL to give hope to all of the New Orleans locals. Evidence of this is the lack of respect that the Saints received during their amazing regular season of 2009. Commentators refused to acknowledge the talent of the 2009 team, even when they went 13-0. When the Saints finally lost to the Dallas Cowboys, most commentators were declaring the Cowboys the best team in the NFC when the season stats were not there to back up the claim. It was almost as if the media felt they had given the Saints a huge push in '05 and were sorely let down. The media didn't seem to come onboard with the Saints until they beat the Brett Favre led Vikings to make it to their first Super Bowl appearance. Not a quantitative analysis, but something interesting to think about.

2005

Week	Date	Opponent	Score
1	11-Sep-05	Carolina Panthers	W 23-20
2	19-Sep-05	New York Giants	L 27-10
3	25-Sep-05	Minnesota Vikings	L 33-16
4	2-Oct-05	Buffalo Bills	W 19-7
5	9-Oct-05	Green Bay Packers	L 52-3
6	16-Oct-05	Atlanta Falcons	L 34-31
7	23-Oct-05	St. Louis Rams	L 28-17
8	30-Oct-05	Miami Dolphins	L 21-6
9	6-Nov-05	Chicago Bears	L 20-17
10	Bye		
11	20-Nov-05	New England Patriots	L 24-17
12	27-Nov-05	New York Jets	W 21-19
13	4-Dec-05	Tampa Bay Buccaneers	L 10-3
14	12-Dec-05	Atlanta Falcons	L 36-17
15	18-Dec-05	Carolina Panthers	L 27-10
16	24-Dec-05	Detroit Lions	L 13-12
17	1-Jan-06	Tampa Bay Buccaneers	L 27-13

2006 – 40TH SEASON

10-6, 1 playoff win, and 1 trip to the NFC Championship Game.

In a bizarre coincidence, the Saints would go to the playoffs in a new head coach's inaugural year for the 2nd time in a row (Haslett in 2000). That's not a stat that most would associate with the long-suffering New Orleans Saints.

Sean Payton was brought in as head coach. Previously, Payton had been a quarterback coach and assistant coach for the Dallas Cowboys.

The Saints took what was considered to be a gamble on Drew Brees by paying him $10 million dollars for his first year when some questioned whether his shoulder injury, which was suffered at the end of the 2005 season while playing for the San Diego Chargers, would hamper his future performance.

The gamble paid off arguably better than any other deal the Saints have ever made. Brees had a fantastic year putting up an astonishing 4,418 yards, which led the league and set a team record, on 356 completions with a 64.3 completion percentage. He had 26 touchdowns with only 11 interceptions.

Deuce McAllister bounced back to have a great year with 244 carries for 1,057 yards averaging 4.3 yards per carry and scoring 10 touchdowns. What makes this more impressive is that for the first time as a Saint, McAllister was sharing a significant number of snaps with rookie Reggie Bush, who ran the ball 155 times. In Bush's rookie year he racked up 565 rushing yards for an average of 3.6 yards per carry. Bush did score on 6 rushing touchdowns.

In the air, the Saints had 4 players catch for over 650 yards each. Marquis Colston led the team with 1,038 yards on 70 receptions. Devery Henderson followed next with 745 yards on 32 catches. Reggie Bush had 88 grabs for 742 yards. And, Joe Horn, while still suffering from injuries managed 679 yards on 37 catches.

John Carney also had a great year nailing 23 of 25 field goal attempts for a 92 FG% and 115 points.

The New Orleans Saints Story 64

The Saints made it to the playoffs and defeated the Philadelphia Eagles 27-24, which was only the 2nd playoff win in team history. The Saints then went to the Conference Championship versus the Chicago Bears in Chicago, but they came up short, losing 14-39.

In a horrible display of sickening behavior, rotten sportsmanship, and a general lack of human decency, a Chicago Bears fan brought a sign to the game that read, "Bears Finishing What Katrina Started." Another said, "In the Flood Noah Saved the Bears not the (picture of the Saints' helmet)." Both of these signs have been verified by Snopes.com as having existed at the game.

Eric Zorn, a *Chicago Tribune* columnist, weighed in on the issue on his blog (http://blogs.chicagotribune.com/news_columnists_ezorn/2007/01/the_silence_of_.html):

"No sports fan could *possibly* be vile and insensitive enough to invoke an ongoing tragedy of the dimensions of Hurricane Katrina–more than 1,200 dead; tens of thousands or more still displaced–to taunt residents of New Orleans. Other fans would have immediately ripped the sign away from him."

Zorn also received this information from a Saints fan who had taken a picture of the Bears fan with the inflammatory sign:

"Unfortunately I had to leave the game early due to threats against me by a Bears fan sitting in front of me...I was also told by that same person that it was too bad I did not drown. Upon leaving the game, I saw a Bears fan throw his beer at a New Orleans TV reporter and then shove him. The next day I was told to ---- off while riding an escalator on the El for wearing a Saints hat. Needless to say, this past Sunday would have been a rough one for Saints fans even if we had won."

In classy and admirable fashion, Zorn responds by apologizing to the Saints fan for his bad experience, and Zorn reminds him that the terrible actions of a few certainly do not represent all Bears fans. Zorn does express his disdain for other Bears fans who did not confront the person with the detestable sign and destroy it.

In short, it was a nasty end to a great season, but it is important to remember that home team fan hostility exists in most stadiums, especially in the postseason, although it certainly does not excuse any of the ugly behavior. It's also key to not ignorantly lump all Bears fans into the same category as the few mentioned here.

On a positive note, Sean Payton won the AP 2006 Coach of the Year Award and the Motorola NFL Coach of the Year Award.

2006

Week	Date	Opponent	Score
1	10-Sep-06	Cleveland Browns	W 19-14
2	17-Sep-06	Green Bay Packers	W 34-27
3	25-Sep-06	Atlanta Falcons	W 23-3
4	1-Oct-06	Carolina Panthers	L 21-18
5	8-Oct-06	Tampa Bay Buccaneers	W 24-21
6	15-Oct-06	Philadelphia Eagles	W 27-24
7	Bye		
8	29-Oct-06	Baltimore Ravens	L 22-35
9	5-Nov-06	Tampa Bay Buccaneers	W 31-14
10	12-Nov-06	Pittsburgh Steelers	L 31-38
11	19-Nov-06	Cincinnati Bengals	L 31-16
12	26-Nov-06	Atlanta Falcons	W 31-13
13	3-Dec-06	San Francisco 49ers	W 34-10
14	10-Dec-06	Dallas Cowboys	W 42-17
15	17-Dec-06	Washington Redskins	L 16-10
16	24-Dec-06	New York Giants	W 30-7
17	31-Dec-06	Carolina Panthers	L 21-31
PLAYOFFS			
Week	Date	Opponent	Score
1	13-Jan-07	Philadelphia Eagles	27-24
2	21-Jan-07	Chicago Bears	39-14

2007 – 41ST SEASON

The New Orleans Saints Story 66

Coming off the fantastic 2006 season, the 7-9 record in 2007 was a disappointment, although there were some great things happening despite the win-loss stats.

Brees had another fantastic year, breaking his own Saints record with 4,423 passing yards on 440 completions (league leading) of 652 passes. Brees had 28 touchdowns and 18 interceptions.

The leader in the air was Marques Colston with 1,202 yards and 11 touchdowns on 98 catches for 12.3 yards per reception average. Next up was David Patten with 792 yards and 3 touchdowns on 54 catches. Reggie Bush caught 73 passes for 417 yards and 2 touchdowns. Devery Henderson grabbed 20 passes for 409 yards and 3 touchdowns.

Reggie Bush ran for 581 yards and 4 touchdowns on 157 carries for a 3.7 yards per carry average. Aaron Stecker had 448 yards and 5 touchdowns on 115 carries for a 3.9 average. Pierre Thomas ran for 252 yards on 52 carries for a 4.8 yard average.

2007

Week	Date	Opponent	Score
1	6-Sep-07	Indianapolis Colts	L 41 - 10
2	16-Sep-07	Tampa Bay Buccaneers	L 31 - 14
3	24-Sep-07	Tennessee Titans	L 31 - 14
4	Bye		
5	7-Oct-07	Carolina Panthers	L 16 - 13
6	14-Oct-07	Seattle Seahawks	W 28 - 17
7	21-Oct-07	Atlanta Falcons	W 22 - 16
8	28-Oct-07	San Francisco 49ers	W 31 - 10
9	4-Nov-07	Jacksonville Jaguars	W 41 - 24
10	11-Nov-07	St. Louis Rams	L 37 - 29
11	18-Nov-07	Houston Texans	L 23 - 10
12	25-Nov-07	Carolina Panthers	W 31 - 6
13	2-Dec-07	Tampa Bay Buccaneers	L 27 - 23

14	10-Dec-07	Atlanta Falcons	W 34 - 14
15	16-Dec-07	Arizona Cardinals	W 31-24
16	23-Dec-07	Philadelphia Eagles	L 38-23
17	30-Dec-07	Chicago Bears	L 33-25

2008 – 42ND SEASON

2008 was not a great year for the Saints, going 8-8, but it was a slight improvement over 2007. However, it was a career year for Drew Brees. Brees led the league with an astonishing 5,069 passing yards (2nd all-time, just 15 yards behind Dan Marino for the best ever), 413 completions, 635 passing attempts, 316.8 average yards per game played, 7.7 net yards gained per pass attempted, and 34 touchdowns. He is also named Offensive Player of the Year.

Pierre Thomas was the rushing leader with 625 yards and 9 touchdowns on 129 carries for a 4.8 yards per carry average. Deuce McAllister in his last season ran for 418 yards and 5 touchdowns on 107 carries for a 3.9 per carry average. Reggie Bush was just behind with 404 yards and 2 touchdowns on 106 carries for a 3.8 average.

The leading receiver was Lance Moore with 928 yards and 10 touchdowns on 79 catches for an 11.7 yards per catch average. Devery Henderson had 793 yards and 3 touchdowns on 32 catches for a 24.8 yards per catch average. Marques Colston had 760 yards and 5 touchdowns on 47 receptions for a 16.2 yards per catch average.

2008

Week	Date	Opponent	Score
1	7-Sep-08	Tampa Bay Buccaneers	W 24-20
2	14-Sep-08	Washington Redskins	L 24-29
3	21-Sep-08	Denver Broncos	L 32-34

The New Orleans Saints Story 68

4	28-Sep-08	San Francisco 49ers	W 31-17
5	6-Oct-08	Minnesota Vikings	L 27-30
6	12-Oct-08	Oakland Raiders	W 34-3
7	19-Oct-08	Carolina Panthers	L 7-30
8	26-Oct-08	San Diego Chargers	W 37-32
9	BYE		
10	9-Nov-08	Atlanta Falcons	L 20-34
11	16-Nov-08	Kansas City Chiefs	W 30-20
12	24-Nov-08	Green Bay Packers	W 51-29
13	30-Nov-08	Tampa Bay Buccaneers	L 23-20
14	7-Dec-08	Atlanta Falcons	W 29-25
15	11-Dec-08	Chicago Bears	L 27-24
16	21-Dec-08	Detroit Lions	W 42-7
17	28-Dec-08	Carolina Panthers	L 31-33

2009 – 43RD SEASON

One could say that it is all too fitting for this magnificent season to have come from the partnership of a quarterback with all the talent in the world who was declared damaged goods several years before by his former team to join with a city with plenty of potential that was labeled as hopeless and beyond repair several years prior.

7 Pro Bowlers were selected from this amazing team: Drew Brees, Jahri Evans, Jon Stinchcomb, Jonathan Goodwin, Darren Sharper, Jonathan Vilma, and Roman Harper. This marked the first year that the NFL set the Pro Bowl to occur during the bye week between the championship games and the Super Bowl. Due to the odd choice on the part of the NFL of putting the game before the Super Bowl, none of these players played in the Pro Bowl.

A game by game, score by score analysis starts in Part II.

2009

Week	Date	Opponent	Score
1	13-Sep-09	Detroit Lions	W 45–27
2	20-Sep-09	at Philadelphia Eagles	W 48–22
3	27-Sep-09	at Buffalo Bills	W 27–7
4	4-Oct-09	New York Jets	W 24–10
5	BYE		
6	18-Oct-09	New York Giants	W 48–27
7	25-Oct-09	at Miami Dolphins	W 46–34
8	2-Nov-09	Atlanta Falcons	W 35–27
9	8-Nov-09	Carolina Panthers	W 30–20
10	15-Nov-09	at St. Louis Rams	W 28–23
11	22-Nov-09	at Tampa Bay Buccaneers	W 38–7
12	30-Nov-09	New England Patriots	W 38–17
13	6-Dec-09	at Washington Redskins	W 33–30
14	13-Dec-09	at Atlanta Falcons	W 26–23
15	19-Dec-09	Dallas Cowboys	L 24–17
16	27-Dec-09	Tampa Bay Buccaneers	L 20-17
17	3-Jan-10	at Carolina Panthers	L 23–10
PLAYOFFS			
Week	Date	Opponent	Score
1	BYE		
2	16-Jan-10	Arizona Cardinals	W 45-14
3	24-Jan-10	Minnesota Vikings	W 31-28
4	7-Feb-10	Indianapolis Colts	W 31-17

PART II: 2009
THE DREAM SEASON

The New Orleans Saints Story 73

WEEK 1 VS. THE DETROIT LIONS

in the Superdome, New Orleans
Date: September 13, 2009

Quarters	1	2	3	4	Total
Lions	3	7	17	0	27
Saints	14	14	10	7	45

1st Quarter: Brees hits 2 touchdown passes to Marques Colston and Robert Meachem. The Lions kick a field goal. Saints lead 14-3 at end of the 1st quarter.

2nd Quarter: Brees hits two more touchdown passes both to Jeremy Shockey. The Lions score on a 4-yard run by Kevin Smith. At the half, Saints lead 28-10.

3rd Quarter: Lions quarterback, Matthew Stafford, scores on a 1-yard touchdown run, and New Orleans answers with a 39-yard John Carney field goal. The Lions would respond with a field goal of their own. Not to be outdone, the Saints hit a touchdown on a 58-yard pass to Devery Henderson. The quarter ends with the Lions returning a fumble for 65 yards and a touchdown. The 3rd quarter is the only one in which the Saints were outscored 17-10, but the Saints lead the game by the margin of 38-27.

4th Quarter: It is the lowest scoring quarter of the game for both teams as the Saints score with 1 touchdown pass to Heath Evans. Final score Saints 45: Lions 27.

GAME NOTES:

Mike Bell was the leading rusher with 143 yards on 28 carries for a 5.11 yards per carry average. Devery Henderson was the leading receiver with 103 yards on 5 receptions. Jeremy Shockey caught 2 touchdown passes.

The Brees Report

Drew Brees becomes the first NFL quarterback to throw 6 touchdown passes in an opening day game. What is even more impressive and telling of the power threat of the Saints offense as a whole is that the 6 touchdowns went to 5 different players: Marques Colston, Robert Meachem, Jeremy Shockey, Devery Henderson, and Heath Evans. On the day, Brees was 26 of 34 for 358 yards with 6 touchdowns and 1 interception.

0-0 Saints Record Going into Game
1-0 Saints Record After Game

WEEK 2 VS. THE PHILADELPHIA EAGLES

in Lincoln Field, Philadelphia
Date: September 20, 2009

Quarters	1	2	3	4	Total
Saints	10	7	17	14	48
Eagles	7	6	7	2	22

1st Quarter: The Saints score 1st on a 15-yard touchdown pass to Marques Colston. The Eagles respond with a 71-yard touchdown pass to DeSean Jackson. The Saints score last in the 1st quarter with John Carney 23-yard field goal. The score at the end of the first was Saints leading 10-7.
2nd Quarter: The Eagles score first with a field goal to tie the game. The Saints reply with a 2nd touchdown pass to Colston. The last points of the half are scored on another Eagles field goal. At the half, Saints lead 17-13.
3rd Quarter: Saints score first in the 2nd half with an 11-yard Heath Evans touchdown reception. Mike Bell runs in a 7-yard touchdown. John Carney kicks a 25-yard field goal, making it 17 unanswered Saints points thus far in the 2nd half. The Eagles score their first and only points in the quarter with a touchdown pass to Jason Avant. At the end of the 3rd, the score was Saints 34: Eagles 23.

4th Quarter: Reggie Bush scores the first touchdown of the last quarter rushing 19 yards into the end zone. Philadelphia mounts an impressive drive to the Saints' 5-yard line, but the Saints red zone defense holds Philadelphia through 4th down, giving the Saints the ball deep in their own territory. Not being able to move forward on their first three downs, the Saints elect to have Brees throw the football out of the end zone to constitute an intentional safety in order to have a better kicking position than from out of their own end zone. The Eagles drive down into Saints territory again but cannot capitalize on it, ending their drive with a Darren Sharper interception that he would run back for a 97-yard touchdown. The final score was Saints 48: Eagles 22.

GAME NOTES:

The Saints outscored the Eagles in all 4 quarters. While the Saints are 2-0, they have allowed an average of 24.5 points to opponents so far this year. Fortunately, the Saints are averaging an astonishing 46.5 points per game on offense. Mike Bell left the game in the 4th quarter with an injury.

The Brees Report

Brees had 3 passing touchdowns on the day, bringing his season total to 9 in just 2 games. He had 311 passing yards on 25 of 34 passes.

1-0 Saints Record Going into Game
2-0 Saints Record After Game

WEEK 3 VS. THE BUFFALO BILLS

in the Ralph Wilson Stadium, New York
Date: September 27, 2009

Quarters	1	2	3	4	Total
Saints	7	3	0	17	27
Bills	0	7	0	0	7

1st Quarter: The Saints make the 1st and only score of the 1st quarter with a 1-yard Lyrell Hamilton TD run. Saints lead 7-0.
2nd Quarter: The Bills pull a fake field goal attempt and kicker Brian Moorman throws a 25-yard pass to Ryan Denney for a touchdown. The Saints score the last points of the quarter with a John Carney field goal. At the half, Saints lead 10-7.
3rd Quarter: The 3rd quarter is scoreless.
4th Quarter: The 4th quarter is all-Saints as Pierre Thomas scores on a 34-yard run, Carney kicks a 35-yard field goal, and Thomas scores again on a 19-yard run. The Saints score 17 points and blank the Bills in the 4th. Final Score Saints 27: Bills 7.

GAME NOTES:

Running back, Pierre Thomas, played his first game of the season, missing the first 2 with a knee injury. Thomas led the team in rushing for 126 yards and 2 touchdowns on 14 carries. The passing game was not as impressive in the first 2 games, and the running game stepped up to cover the difference. Colston did manage to receive 4 passes for 67 yards, followed by Shockey with 6 receptions for 48 yards. Thus far in the season, the Saints have scored 1st in all 3 games and have never been losing to an opponent at any time.

The Brees Report

Brees threw for 172 yards on 16 of 29 attempts with no passing touchdowns.

2-0 Saints Record Going into Game
3-0 Saints Record After Game

WEEK 4 VS. THE NEW YORK JETS

in the Superdome, New Orleans
Date: October 4, 2009

The New Orleans Saints Story 77

Quarters	1	2	3	4	Total
Jets	0	3	7	0	10
Saints	3	14	0	7	24

1st Quarter: John Carney kicks a field goal for the Saints to score first. At the end of the 1st, Saints lead 3-0.

2nd Quarter: Safety Darren Sharper intercepts a pass and returns it 99 yards for a touchdown. Defensive End Will Smith causes a fumble in the Buffalo end zone which is covered by Saints defensive tackle Remi Ayodele for 7 points. New York's Jay Feely kicks a 38-yard field goal for the last points of the quarter. At the half, Saints lead 14-3.

3rd Quarter: The Jets score first on a Thomas Jones 15-yard run for a touchdown. The Saints do not score in the 3rd quarter, but lead at its end 17-10.

4th Quarter: Pierre Thomas is the lone touchdown of the 4th quarter, bringing the final score of Saints 24: Jets 10.

GAME NOTES:

Even though the Saints win by a strong 14 points, it was the closest game of the season thus far. Thomas rushed for 88 yards on 19 carries and 1 touchdown with a 4.63 yards per carry average. Thomas also led in receiving with 46 yards on 4 receptions.

The Brees Report

Brees threw for 190 yards on 20 of 32 pass attempts with no passing touchdowns.

3-0 Saints Record Going into Game
4-0 Saints Record After Game

Week 5 - Bye Week
Date: October 11, 2009

Week 6 vs. The New York Giants
in the Superdome, New Orleans
Date: October 18, 2009

Quarters	1	2	3	4	Total
Giants	3	14	0	10	27
Saints	14	20	7	7	48

1st Quarter: The scoring began for the Saints with a 2-yard touchdown run. Soon after Jeremy Shockey caught a 1-yard pass for a touchdown. The Giants managed to kick a field goal before the end of the quarter, making the score 14-3 in favor of the Saints.

2nd Quarter: Robert Meachem scores on a 36-yard touchdown pass from Brees. The Giants respond with an Ahmad Bradshaw rushing touchdown. Brees then hits Lance Moore for a 12-yard touchdown. In kind, the Giants score on a 15-yard pass to Mario Manningham. The Saints score the final points of the half with a 7-yard rushing touchdown from Reggie Bush, leaving the score with the Saints leading 34-17.

3rd Quarter: The only score of the quarter is another Saints touchdown on a Brees to Marques Colston 12-yard pass. End of the 3rd, Saints winning 41-17.

4th Quarter: Giants score first with a Tynes field goal from 38 yards out. The Saints retaliate with a Heath Evans 2-yard touchdown. With Eli Manning out of the game, David Carr throws a touchdown pass to Hakeem Nicks for the last points of the game. Final Saints 48: Giants 27.

Game Notes:

Going into the game, the Giants were 5-0 and had the #1 defense in overall defense and pass defense. In the first 5 games of the season, the Giants had held opponents to an average of 14.2 points per game. The Saints not only tripled that figure by the end of the game, but had more than doubled it by the half. This win against Eli Manning and the undefeated Giants marked a turning point in winning over some of the press who were still trying to write off the Saints' success as a fluke. Some analysts had picked the Giants to be in the Super Bowl, so this win made some people take notice of the Saints' potential.

Pierre Thomas rushed for 72 yards on 15 carries, followed by Mike Bell who ran for 34 yards on 15 carries. Marcus Colston had a great game receiving 8 passes for 166 yards and an impressive 20.8 average yards per catch. Next up was Lance Moore with 78 yards on 6 catches.

Eli Manning was held to 1 passing touchdown on the day.

4 games into the season, and the Saints have still never been losing at any point in any game.

The Brees Report
Brees had an amazing game with 369 passing yards on 23 of 30 pass attempts with 4 touchdowns.

4-0 Saints Record Going into Game
5-0 Saints Record After Game

WEEK 7 VS. THE MIAMI DOLPHINS
in the Landshark Stadium, FL
Date: October 25, 2009

Quarters	1	2	3	4	Total
Saints	3	7	14	22	46
Dolphins	14	10	10	0	34

The Dream Season 80

1st Quarter: Former Saint Ricky Williams scores on a 4-yard touchdown run on 1 play following a Brees interception. The Saints score with a 47-yard field goal by Carney. Williams scores again on a 68-yard TD run. At the end of the 1st quarter, the Saints were trailing 14-3.

2nd Quarter: Brees is intercepted again. Dolphins kick a field goal. Ronnie Brown rushes for a touchdown for the Dolphins. Brees throws a pass to Colston which is deemed down at the ½ yard line. Brees convinces Coach Payton to go for the touchdown, and the quarterback dives over the line himself to score the touchdown. At the half, the Saints were down 24-10.

3rd Quarter: Darren Sharper makes an interception and runs it back for a Saints touchdown. The ball is knocked out of Brees' hand as he tries to throw a pass, and the Dolphins get the ball, resulting in a field goal. Brees hits Colston for a touchdown. Ricky Williams rushes for his 3rd touchdown of the day. At the end of the 3rd quarter, the Saints were down 24-34.

4th Quarter: Reggie Bush dives through the air the last 5 yards for a touchdown. Drew Brees runs the ball in for another touchdown, giving the Saints their 1st lead in the game, despite Carney missing an extra point. Tracy Porter intercepts a pass and runs it back for a touchdown. The Saints win 46-34.

GAME NOTES:

This game marks the first time during the season that the Saints were ever losing to an opponent at any time.

Bell was the leading rusher for the Saints with 80 yards on 12 carries. Next up was Pierre Thomas with 30 yards on 8 carries. In the air, Shockey was the leading receiver with 105 yards on 4 receptions. Colston had 72 yards on 5 grabs.

2 of the Saints' touchdowns were scored by the defense.

Former Saint Ricky Williams had 3 touchdowns on the day.

The Brees Report

Brees threw for 298 yards on 22 of 38 pass attempts for 1 touchdown and 3 interceptions (highest so far in the season for Brees). Brees was sacked 5 times.

5-0 Saints Record Going into Game
6-0 Saints Record After Game

WEEK 8 VS. THE ATLANTA FALCONS

in the Superdome, New Orleans
Date: November 2, 2009

Quarters	1	2	3	4	Total
Falcons	14	0	7	6	27
Saints	7	21	0	7	35

1st Quarter: The scoring started for Atlanta with a 13-yard run for a touchdown by Michael Turner. The Saints would respond in kind with a 22-yard touchdown run from Pierre Thomas. The Falcons sack Drew Brees causing a fumble which is ran in for a 4-yard Falcons touchdown by Kroy Biermann. At the end of the 1st quarter, Falcons lead 14-7.

2nd Quarter: Brees to Colston for 18-yards and a touchdown. Reggie Bush runs a 1-yarder in for a touchdown. Jabaru Greer intercepts and runs for 48-yards and another Saints touchdown. Atlanta's offense was shut out of the 2nd quarter. At the half, Saints led 28-14.

3rd Quarter: Falcons score first in the 2nd half with a Matt Ryan 68-yard touchdown pass to Roddy White to narrow the Saints' lead to 1 touchdown.

4th Quarter: The Falcons's Jason Elam kicks a 25-yard field goal. Tracy Porter intercepts to give the Saints the ball, and Brees hits Pierre Thomas with a 1-yard pass for a touchdown. The Falcons score last with a 40-yard field goal. The Falcons attempt

The Dream Season 82

and recover an onside kick. However, Darren Sharper intercepts and ends their drive.

GAME NOTES:

This game was the Saints' 1st Monday Night Football win in their last 4 contests. This marks only the 2nd game so far in the season in which the Saints have ever been losing, although it is the second game in a row that it has happened. The Saints' 7-0 record ties their best start ever, which happened back in 1991 with Coach Jim Mora and QB Bobby Hebert.

Besides catching a touchdown pass and running in another touchdown, Pierre Thomas was the rushing leader with 91 yards on 14 carries for an impressive 6.5 yards per carry average. Bell was next with 49 yards on 17 carries.

In the air, Colston was the leader with 85 yards on 6 receptions. Shockey was next in line with 72 yards on 5 grabs.

The Brees Report

Brees went 25 of 33 for 308 yards and 2 touchdowns with 2 interceptions.

6-0 Saints Record Going into Game
7-0 Saints Record After Game

WEEK 9 VS. THE CAROLINA PANTHERS

in the Superdome, New Orleans
Date: November 8, 2009

Quarters	1	2	3	4	Total
Panthers	14	3	3	0	20
Saints	0	6	14	10	30

The New Orleans Saints Story 83

1st Quarter: The Carolina Panthers score the only points in the 1st quarter with a 66-yard touchdown run by DeAngelo Williams. The fleet-footed Williams scores a 2nd touchdown on a 7-yard run. At the end of the 1st quarter, Panthers lead 14-0.

2nd Quarter: Saints finally get on the board with a Carney 23-yard field goal. The Panthers respond with a Kasay 25-yard field goal of their own, hanging on to their 14-point lead. The Saints kick a 2nd field goal. At the end of the half, Saints still trail 17-6.

3rd Quarter: The Saints get into the end zone for the 1st time with a Pierre Thomas 10-yard rushing touchdown. The Panthers put up a 25-yard field goal. The Saints score again with a Robert Meachem 54-yard touchdown reception. At the end of the 3rd, the Saints have tied the game at 20-20.

4th Quarter: The 4th quarter belongs to the Saints. The first score is a Carney 40-yard field goal. The last points of the game are scored by the Saints on a defensive forced fumble that is picked up by Anthony Hargrove for a 1-yard touchdown. Final score: Saints 30-Falcons 20.

GAME NOTES:

For the 3rd game in a row, the Saints came from behind to win. The Saints advanced to an 8-0 record, the best start in franchise history.

On the ground Pierre Thomas ran for 50 yards on 13 carries and 1 touchdown. Bell was next with 17 yards on 5 carries.

In the air Robert Meachem caught 5 passes for 98 yards, and Henderson had 3 grabs for 93 yards.

The Brees Report

Brees threw 24 completions on 35 attempts for 330 yards and 1 touchdown.

7-0 Saints Record Going into Game
8-0 Saints Record After Game

Week 10 vs. The St. Louis Rams

in the Edward Jones Dome, St. Louis
Date: November 15, 2009

Quarters	1	2	3	4	Total
Saints	0	14	7	7	28
Rams	0	14	3	6	23

1st Quarter: No score in the first quarter.
2nd Quarter: Reggie Bush scores on a 3-yard touchdown run to put the Saints on the board. The Rams also score a touchdown on a 28-yard pass to Donnie Avery. Bush scores again, but this time on a 15-yard Drew Brees pass. To make the quarter a perfect see-saw battle, the Rams score another touchdown on a Steven Jackson 2-yard run. At the half, the Saints are tied 14-14.
3rd Quarter: The Saints score on the opening kickoff with Courtney Roby dashing off for a 97-yard touchdown run. The Rams kick a 32-yard field goal courtesy of Josh Brown. At the end of the 3rd, the Saints have taken the lead 21-17.
4th Quarter: Drew Brees finds Robert Meachem in the end zone with a 37-yard pass. The Rams score on a 19-yard pass to Bulger, but they attempt and fail to make a 2-point conversion.

Game Notes:

Saints advance to 9-0. The Saints won by 5 points, which is their closest game played so far this year based on final score.

Reggie Bush was the leading rusher with 83 yards on 6 carries for an impressive 13.8 yards per carry avg. Meachem was 2nd with 41 yards on 1 carry.

Receiving leader was Henderson with 72 yards on 4 grabs, followed by David Thomas with 45 yards on 5 receptions.

The Brees Report

Brees connected on 18 of 26 passes for 223 yards and 2 touchdowns.

The New Orleans Saints Story 85

8-0 Saints Record Going into Game
9-0 Saints Record After Game

Week 11 vs. The Tampa Bay Buccaneers

in the Raymond James Stadium, Tampa, FL
Date: November 22, 2009

Quarters	1	2	3	4	Total
Saints	7	10	14	7	38
Buccaneers	7	0	0	0	7

1st Quarter: The Buccaneers score 1st with a touchdown pass from Josh Freeman to Michael Clayton. Robert Meachem caught a 4-yard touchdown pass, evening the score at 7-7 at the end of the 1st.

2nd Quarter: The Saints put up 3 points on a Carney field goal to take the lead. Meachem makes his 2nd touchdown reception, this one for 6-yards. At the half, it's Saints leading 17-7.

3rd Quarter: The Bucs fumble away their 1st possession of the half, which leads to a Drew Brees to David Thomas touchdown reception, which is Thomas's first as a Saint. At the end of the 3rd, the Saints lead 31-7.

4th Quarter: Mike Bell dives into the end zone for a Saints touchdown for the only score of the 4th quarter.

Game Notes:

The Saints move to 10-0.
    Pierre Thomas had a good day racking up 92 yards on 11 carries. Mike Bell hit 75 yards on 13 carries for 2 touchdowns.

for 74 yards. David Thomas had 4 grabs for 66 yards and 1 touchdown.

The Saints defense contributed greatly in this game. Although the Bucs scored first, the Saints defense would prevent them from doing so again for the rest of the game. Saints D also picked off 3 passes for interceptions.

The Brees Report
Drew Brees threw 19 completions of 29 attempts for 187 yards and 3 touchdowns. It was one of Brees's lower yardage games, but he rocketed 3 passes in the end zone for touchdowns.

9-0 Saints Record Going into Game
10-0 Saints Record After Game

WEEK 12 VS. THE NEW ENGLAND PATRIOTS
in the Superdome, New Orleans
Date: November 30, 2009

Quarters	1	2	3	4	Total
Patriots	7	3	7	0	17
Saints	3	21	7	7	38

1st Quarter: The Saints start off with a 30-yard John Carney field goal. The Patriots take the lead with a 4-yard touchdown run by Laurence Maroney. At the end of the 1st, Saints trail 3-7.
2nd Quarter: Brady is intercepted by Mike McKenzie, which gave Brees the opportunity to hit Pierre Thomas on an 18-yard touchdown pass to take the lead. Brees throws a 75-yard touchdown pass to Henderson. The Pats put up 3 on a 38-yard field goal by Stephen Gostkowski. Meachem catches a 38-yard touchdown reception from Drew Brees. The half ends with Pats'

The New Orleans Saints Story 87

kicker Gostkowski missing a 50-yard field goal attempt, leaving the score at 24-10, Saints 2 touchdowns in the lead.

3rd Quarter: Pats score on a second Maroney rushing touchdown, this one for 2-yards. The Saints score on a 2-yard nab by Darnell Dinkins. After 3 quarters, the Saints lead 31-17.

4th Quarter: Colston catches Brees's 5th touchdown pass of the day. Sharper picks off his 8th interception of the year. Brady is yanked off the field, and Brad Hoyer finishes the game. Final score is Saints with a whopping 38 points to the Pats' 17.

GAME NOTES:

The Saints moved onto 11-0 with another Monday Night victory.

This game was a telling one for the Saints as many analysts considered it to be the most challenging matchup for them all year.

The Saints defense had 2 interceptions and prevented Tom Brady from making a single touchdown pass. Brady on the day was 21 of 36 for 237 yards.

Pierre Thomas had 11 carries for 64 yards, averaging 5.8 yards on each. Mike Bell racked up 50 yards on 13 runs.

Colston was the leading receiver with 121 yards on 4 receptions, averaging 30 yards per catch and 1 touchdown, and Henderson made 3 grabs for 116 yards, averaging 38.7 on each, and scoring a touchdown.

The Brees Report

5 passing touchdowns tell the tale of the day for the Saints. Brees accomplished the 5 end zone completions on 18 completions of 23 attempts for an impressive 371 yards. To top it off, he did all of it without a single interception.

10-0 Saints Record Going into Game
11-0 Saints Record After Game

The Dream Season 88

Week 13 vs. The Washington Redskins

in FedEx Field, Maryland
Date: December 6, 2009

Quarters	1	2	3	4	OT	Total
Saints	0	17	3	10	3	33
Redskins	10	7	10	3	0	30

1st Quarter: The Redskins get on the scoreboard 1st on an 8-yard touchdown throw from Jason Campbell to Fred Davis. Next, Washington's Shaun Shuisham kicks a 32-yard field goal. After 1 quarter, the Saints are down 10-0.

2nd Quarter: Garrett Hartley kicks a 34-yard field goal. Next, the Saints score on a 40-yard touchdown reception to Colston to tie the game. The Redskins charge back with a Devin Thomas 10-yard touchdown catch to retake the lead. Brees throws the ball to Jeremy Shockey but is intercepted by Kareem Moore. However, Meachem strips the newly intercepted ball out of Moore's hands and returns it 44-yards for a Saints touchdown. At the half, the Saints have tied the score 17-17.

3rd Quarter: Suisham hits a 28-yard field goal for Washington. The Redskins put more points on the board with a 13-yard touchdown pass to Devin Thomas. Hartley kicks another field goal for the Saints from 27 yards out. At the end of 3, the Saints are behind 20-27.

4th Quarter: Hartley and Suisham both kick field goals, and both take turns missing a field goal in this quarter. The Saints make a lightning fast 33-second drive down the field to hit Meachem for the tying touchdown on a 53-yard reception from Drew Brees. The Saints intercept the ball and gain a chance to win the game. Hartley is given the opportunity to kick a game-winning 58-yard field goal. The kick is very short and does not make it. At the end of the 4th quarter, the game is tied at 30-30, heading into overtime.

Overtime: The Saints take the lead for the 1st time in the game and win the contest on an 18-yard Garrett Hartley field goal.

The New Orleans Saints Story 89

GAME NOTES:
The Saints move to 12-0.
   Mike Bell led the ground assault with 34 yards on 16 carries. Pierre Thomas had 18 yards on 6 carries. This was certainly a passing game.
   Meachem caught for 142 yards and 1 TD on 8 grabs. Pierre Thomas also caught 8 passes for 64 yards.

The Brees Report
Brees passes for over 400 yards for the 5th time in his career. The exact number was 419 yards on 35 completions of 49 attempts for 2 touchdowns and 1 interception.

11-0 Saints Record Going into Game
12-0 Saints Record After Game

WEEK 14 VS. THE ATLANTA FALCONS
in the Georgia Dome, Atlanta
Date: December 13, 2009

Quarters	1	2	3	4	Total
Saints	3	13	7	3	26
Falcons	6	3	7	7	23

1st Quarter: The Falcons strike first blood with a 36-yard Matt Bryant field goal. The Saints put up a field goal of their own via Garret Hartley from 33 yards out. Truly being a quarter of the kickers, Atlanta puts 3 more points on the board with another Bryant field goal, this one from 30 yards. At the end of 1, Saints trail 3-6.
2nd Quarter: The Saints get into the end zone with a 6-yard Reggie Bush run to take the lead. Racking up another touchdown, Drew Brees finds Marquis Colston on a 3-yard touchdown pass.

The Dream Season 90

However, Hartley misses the extra point. The Falcons kick their 3rd field goal of the day, Bryant sailing the ball between the uprights from 27 yards out. At the half, Saints lead 19-9.

3rd Quarter: Reggie Bush catches a 21-yard Drew Brees pass for a touchdown. The Falcons get into the end zone themselves with a 50-yard touchdown reception from Chris Redman to Michael Jenkins.

4th Quarter: Following up with another score is the Falcons on a 4-yard rush by Jason Snelling, tying the game. The Saints get a 38-yard field goal from the foot of Garrett Hartley to regain the lead. The Saints get an interception courtesy of Jonathan Vilma. Trying to extend their lead, the Saints attempt a fake field goal, but turn the ball over.

GAME NOTES:

The Saints reach the pinnacle of their unbeaten streak going to 13-0, which earns them a 1st-round bye in the playoffs.

The Saints defense made some key stops but gave up 392 yards on the day. Opposing quarterback Redman passed for 303 yards and 1 touchdown on 23 of 34 throws.

Leading rusher Pierre Thomas had 47 yards on 13 carries, and Reggie Bush had 33 yards on 6 runs. Bush had 2 touchdowns, but as a receiver, not as a rusher.

The airborne leaders were Robert Meachem with 57 yards on 4 receptions and Marques Colston with 54 yards on 6 grabs for 1 touchdown.

The Brees Report

Brees threw for 296 yards on 31 of 40 attempts with 3 touchdowns.

12-0 Saints Record Going into Game
13-0 Saints Record After Game

WEEK 15 VS. THE DALLAS COWBOYS
in the Superdome, New Orleans

The New Orleans Saints Story 91

Date: December 19, 2009

Quarters	1	2	3	4	Total
Cowboys	14	3	7	0	24
Saints	0	3	0	14	17

1st Quarter: The first quarter belonged to the Cowboys. Their first score is on a 49-yard pass to Miles Austin. Their second score is on a Marion Baber 3-yard touchdown run. After 1, the Saints trail 0-14.

2nd Quarter: Garrett Hartley sends 1 between the uprights from 34 yards out for the Saints' first 3 points of the game and only points of the half. The Cowboys respond with a 44-yard field goal of their own from the foot of Nick Folk, ending the half with the Saints losing 3-17.

3rd Quarter: The Cowboys take the only points of the 3rd quarter with a 2-yard touchdown run by Marion Barber for his 2nd end zone run of the day.

4th Quarter: The 4th quarter was all-Saints starting with a Mike Bell 1-yard touchdown run. The Saints defense sends the Cowboys 3 downs and out, and Brees zings a 7-yard touchdown pass to Lance Moore, bringing the Saints within 1 score of tying the game. The Cowboys drive down to the Saints' 8-yard line, but the Saints defense holds them to a field goal attempt, which is missed at 24 yards out. With 10 seconds left, the Saints have their opportunity to tie the game, but Brees is sacked which forces a fumble that is picked up by the Cowboys' Jay Ratliff. The Cowboys kneel the ball to run out the clock.

GAME NOTES:

The Cowboys deliver the Saints their first loss of the season in this Saturday game. This game also marks the 1st time this season that the Saints did not score at least 3 touchdowns. Reggie Bush was injured in the 2nd quarter and did not return to the game. The Saints offensive line allowed 4 sacks during the game, which was a season high, having only allowed 15 sacks total in all previous 13 games this season.

The Dream Season 92

Reggie Bush was the leading rusher with 29 yards on 1 carry, followed by Pierre Thomas with 20 yards on 6 carries. On the receiving end, Marques Colston had 86 yards on 5 receptions, and David Thomas picked up 77 yards on 8 grabs.

It is notable that the Saints only lost by 1 touchdown in their only loss thus far in the season.

The Brees Report
Brees throws for 298 yards in the game, which gives him his 4th consecutive 4,000+ yard season. The only other NFL player to have accomplished this milestone is the Colts' Peyton Manning. Brees was sacked 4 times during the game.

13-0 Saints Record Going into Game
13-1 Saints Record After Game

Week 16 vs. The Tampa Bay Buccaneers
in the Superdome, New Orleans
Date: December 27, 2009

Quarters	1	2	3	4	OT	Total
Buccaneers	0	3	0	14	3	20
Saints	14	3	0	0	0	17

1st Quarter: The Saints get on the board first with a Pierre Thomas rushing touchdown. Darren Sharper intercepts, and it sets up a Drew Brees to Marques Colston touchdown reception. At the end of the 1st quarter, the Saints are shutting out the Bucs 14-0.

2nd Quarter: The Saints get 3 more points on a 28-yard Hartley field goal. The Bucs counter with a 34-yard field goal by Barth. At the half, the Saints lead 17-3.

3rd Quarter: No score in the 3rd quarter.

4th Quarter: The Bucs score on a 23-yard run by Cadillac Williams. The Bucs get in the end zone again with a punt return for a touchdown by Michael Spurlock, tying the game at 17. The Saints drive downfield and try to win the game with a Hartley field goal from 37 yards out. Unfortunately the kick misses, which forces overtime.

Overtime: The Bucs do exactly what the Saints failed to do at the end of the 4th quarter. They drive downfield and kick a game-winning 47-yard field goal, defeating the Saints 20-17.

GAME NOTES:

The Saints lose their 2nd game of the season which happens to be the 2nd loss in a row.

The rushing leader for the Saints was Pierre Thomas for 60 yards on 6 runs with 1 touchdown. Despite being the team rushing leader of the game, Thomas was injured with bruised ribs and did not return to play. Next up was Lynell Hamilton, who had 21 yards on 7 carries.

The leading New Orleans receivers were Marquis Colston with 77 yards on 8 catches and Meachem with 66 yards on 5 grabs.

On defense Darren Sharper's interception in this game was the 63rd on his career, placing him tied for 6th place on the all-time interception list.

Despite Sharper's accomplishment, the Saints defense did not have a good day allowing Tampa Bay's Cadillac Williams alone to rush for 129 yards.

The Brees Report

Brees threw for 258 yards on 32 completions of 37 attempts for 1 touchdown. Even though the Saints had their 2nd loss in a row, Brees's completion ratio was an astounding 86.48% on the day.

13-1 Saints Record Going into Game
13-2 Saints Record After Game

Week 17 vs. The Carolina Panthers

in the Bank of America Stadium, NC
Date: January 3, 2010

Quarters	1	2	3	4	Total
Saints	0	3	7	0	10
Panthers	7	10	6	0	23

1st Quarter: The Panthers score first with a 67-yard touchdown run by Jonathan Stewart. After 1, the Saints are behind 0-7.
2nd Quarter: Garrett Hartley kicks a 35-yard field goal to give the Saints their first 3 points of the game. Carolina's Matt Moore hits Dwayne Jarrett with a 30-yard touchdown pass. The Panthers add to their lead with the last points of the half in a John Kasay 41-yard field goal. At the half, the Saints are down by 2 touchdowns with a score of 3-17.
3rd Quarter: The 3rd quarter belongs to Carolina kicker, John Kasay, who scored twice on field goals from 39 and 37 yards.
4th Quarter: The last quarter of the season is scoreless, giving the Panthers the win with a final tally of 23-10 over the Saints.

Game Notes:

The season ends with the Saints losing their 3rd straight, but finishing 13-3.

Expectations for the Saints in this last game of the season were not high as Drew Brees and other starters were being benched to keep them safe and healthy for the postseason. Benching the starting quarterback was a move that was controversial among fans and pundits, but it was the same strategy used by the Indianapolis Colts. In the particular case of these 2 teams, the criticism and concern of fans and experts were for naught as both organizations made it to the Super Bowl. The Saints had nothing to gain in this last game of the regular season as they had already solidified being the #1 seed in the NFC and gaining home field advantage.

The New Orleans Saints Story 95

The statistic that no NFL team has ever made the Super Bowl after losing the last 3 games of the season was touted often by sportscasters, but the Saints proved them wrong.

One of the down points of the game was Saints kick returner Courtney Roby getting injured in the 2nd quarter and not returning to the game.

The Brees Report

He looked good from the bench. Seriously, sitting out this game may have been a crucial ingredient to the Saints' postseason success. Having won the Super Bowl, it surely didn't hurt anything.

Brees's backup, Mark Brunell, did not have a good game. He threw for a total of 102 yards, completing 15 of 29 passes with no passing touchdowns. Considering how little game time Brunell has seen with the Saints behind starter Drew Brees, it's hard to be very critical.

13-2 Saints Record Going into Game
13-3 Saints Record After Game

WEEK 18
Playoffs Week 1 - Wild Card - BYE
Date: January 9-10, 2010

WEEK 19 VS. THE ARIZONA CARDINALS
Playoffs Week 2 - NFC Divisional Round
in the Superdome, New Orleans
Date: January 16, 2010

Quarters	1	2	3	4	Total
Cardinals	7	7	0	0	14
Saints	21	14	10	0	45

The Dream Season 96

1st Quarter: The Cardinals strike first blood with a 70-yard touchdown run by Tim Hightower. The Saints answer quickly with a 1-yard touchdown run by Lynell Hamilton. A Drew Brees 17-yard touchdown pass to Jeremy Shockey would be the Saints' 2nd score of the quarter. Still not finished, Reggie Bush runs 54 yards for a TD. After 1, Saints lead 21-7.

2nd Quarter: Arizona scores first again with a 4-yard touchdown run by Chris Wells. The Saints fire right back with a 44-yard touchdown reception by Devery Henderson. Adding 1 more score to their total before half time, the Saints score on a 2-yard Drew Brees to Marques Colston touchdown pass. At the half, Saints dominate 35-14.

3rd Quarter: Garrett Hartley nails a 43-yard field goal for New Orleans. Reggie Bush scores again on an impressive 83-yard punt return touchdown. After 3, Saints lead 45-14.

4th Quarter: The 4th quarter is scoreless, sending the Saints to the NFC Championship Game versus the Minnesota Vikings.

GAME NOTES:

The Saints did exactly what they had done earlier in the year and exactly what fans were hoping for in getting ahead of the Cardinals early on. The game was essentially over in the 1st quarter as the Saints scored 21 points, and the Cardinals only scored 14 points on the game and none in the 2nd half.

Leading rushing for the Saints was Reggie Bush with 84 yards on 5 carries for 1 touchdown and a stunning 16.8 yards per carry average. Bush also had a touchdown on an 83-yard punt return. Behind Bush was Pierre Thomas with 13 carries for 52 yards.

Yardage was split almost evenly between receivers with Colston catching 6 passes for 83 yards and 1 touchdown and Henderson grabbing 4 for 80 yards and 1 touchdown.

The New Orleans Saints Story 97

The Brees Report
Drew Brees passed for 23 of 32 and 247 yards and 3 touchdowns, silencing critics who thought he may be rusty following the bye week and sitting out the last game of the season the week before.

13-3 Saints Record Going into Game
14-3 Saints Record After Game

WEEK 20 VS. THE MINNESOTA VIKINGS
Playoffs Week 3 – NFC Championship Game
in the Superdome, New Orleans
Date: January 24, 2010

Quarters	1	2	3	4	OT	Total
Vikings	14	0	7	7	0	28
Saints	7	7	7	7	3	31

1st Quarter: The Vikings get on the board first with a 19-yard touchdown run by Adrian Peterson. The Saints answer quickly with a Drew Brees 38-yard touchdown pass to Pierre Thomas. Minnesota gets the last score of the quarter with a 9-yard Farve pass to Sidney Rice. After the 1st quarter, Saints trail 7-14.

2nd Quarter: The Saints own the 2nd quarter, scoring the only points on a 9-yard Drew Brees to Devery Henderson reception for a touchdown. At the half, the Saints & Vikings were tied 14-14.

3rd Quarter: Pierre Thomas scores 1st in the 2nd half on a 9-yard touchdown run, giving the Saints their first lead in the game. The Vikings answer with a 1-yard touchdown run by Peterson. After 3 quarters, the game was tied again, 21-21.

4th Quarter: The Saints take the lead again with a 5-yard Brees to Bush touchdown pass. The Vikings even the score up again

The Dream Season 98

with an Adrian Peterson 2-yard touchdown run. At the end of the 2nd half, the game was tied at 28-28, forcing overtime.

Overtime: Garrett Hartley, blamed by Saints' fans for the loss against Tampa Bay in Week 16, becomes an instant hero as he kicks a 40-yard game-winning field goal, sending the Saints to their first Super Bowl in franchise history.

GAME NOTES:

In a tight overtime game, Saints fans were thinking to many days of old in which leads were lost in the end and hopes were raised only to be dashed. However, the 2009 Saints team was a different beast altogether, one that chose to fight until the last second of every game, never surrendering to negative psychology of which past teams have seemed susceptible.

For starters the Saints became the 1st team to reach the Super Bowl after losing the final 3 games of the season. On top of just making it there, they won the Super Bowl against a magnificent Colts team. No one had done that before, and before the playoffs many sportscasters were claiming that the Saints were not likely to make it to the big game either. What that often quoted gris-gris on the Saints ignores is how many of those teams that made up that stat were 13-0 when they lost the remaining 3 games of the season. And, furthermore, how many of them benched their starters in the final game? And lastly, how many of them had the #1 offense in the league in many categories? The naysayers were a bit blind in putting too much weight in that statistic. They should have placed more stock in comparing the Saints' season accomplishments with those of the other teams entering the playoffs after losing their last 3 games. After all, the Saints only lost by 7 and 3 in the games before benching their starters, which means they were always within 1 strike of tying or winning both of their losses with their starters.

Leading rushers for the Saints are Pierre Thomas with 61 yards and 1 touchdown on 14 carries. Reggie Bush was 2nd in line with only 8 yards on 7 carries.

In the air, Devery Henderson had 39 yards on 4 receptions with 1 touchdown, and Pierre Thomas had 38 yards and 1 touchdown on 2 catches.

The Brees Report
Brees threw for 197 yards and 3 touchdowns on 17 of 30 attempts.

14-3 Saints Record Going into Game
15-3 Saints Record After Game

Super Bowl XLIV

Week 21 vs. The Indianapolis Colts

Playoffs Week 4 – Super Bowl XLIV
in the Sun Life Stadium, Miami, FL
Date: February 7, 2010

Pre-Game Information:
The 2 #1 seeds met each other for the first time in 19 years since The Dallas Cowboys met The Buffalo Bills in Super Bowl XXVIII, and it was only the 3rd time in NFL history that it has happened. Going into the game, the Saints' record was 15-3, and the Colts' record was 16-2. Both teams did not play their starters in the last regulation game of the season. The Saints went 13-0 without losing a game, and the Colts went 14-0 before their first loss.

For the 1st time in Super Bowl history, 2 quarterbacks were facing each other with over 4,000 yards a piece during the season.

Going into the game, not many experts picked the Saints to win. The common cop-out response was, "I'm picking the Colts with my brain and the Saints with my heart." That response is an insult to the Saints' talent, implying that they were not equipped to compete with Peyton Manning and the Colts and that no one could seriously think the Saints could win. If one can't

The Dream Season 100

imagine in one's brain that the Saints could win, one is making the statement that the Saints do not have a logical chance. When they say they can only hope for a Saints win in their hearts and not their heads, they are saying they are wishing beyond logic for an ill-equipped team to have a miracle, and that only the foolhardy could believe in it. That is the way one would describe a contest of the NFL Super Bowl Champions playing a non-talented 9-year-olds playground team; it is no way to discuss a team with the record and statistics of the 2009 New Orleans Saints. The teams with the best 2 records in all of football were meeting. Of course, both teams had a conceivable chance of winning.

One of the few experts to give the Saints credit was Michael Irving, and he also expressed his disdain for the lack of coverage and respect that the media were handing the Saints, "We've talked a great deal about a number of things and missed what we should be talking about. And I don't mind telling you that I have been upset with our coverage of the New Orleans Saints in this Super Bowl Bid. This is ENORMOUS for them!....this bid is going towards the infrastructure of that city....The Monday paper has sold out. They printed it again Tuesday; it sold out again. They are talking about reprinting it again, and it will sell out again, that tells you what that means to those people. And we have done a great disservice to this city."

On behalf of New Orleans, thank you, Michael.

Out of ESPN's panel of 37, 25 picked the Colts to win, and only 12 selected the Saints. Not only were all 25 wrong, but they were wrong by at least 2 touchdowns as the Saints won by 14 points. So had they picked the Colts to win by 7, they were off by 21 points in their Super Bowl picks. While it's true that any team in the NFL can beat any other team on a given day, the inaccurate landslide voting of the panel illustrates the lack of credit given to the Saints in favor of the media darling Colts and Peyton Manning.

Specifically speaking the chart below shows the predictions and how far they were off reality as taken from http://www.espnmediazone3.com/us/2010/02/super-bowl-xliv-predictions-from-espn/.

The New Orleans Saints Story 101

Panelist	Predicted Winner	Win By	Off By
Marcellus Wiley	Colts	15	29
Mike Greenberg	Colts	14	28
Steve Levy	Colts	13	27
Trey Wingo	Colts	13	27
Tom Jackson	Colts	11	25
Kenny Mayne	Colts	11	25
Sal Paolantonio	Colts	11	25
Russell Baxter	Colts	11	25
Chris Berman	Colts	10	24
Gary Horton	Colts	10	24
Adam Schefter	Colts	10	24
Michele Tafoya	Colts	8	22
Mike Tirico	Colts	8	22
Mike Golic	Colts	7	21
Mark Schlereth	Colts	7	21
Colin Cowherd	Colts	6	20
Chris Mortensen	Colts	6	20
Michael Wilbon	Colts	6	20
Matthew Berry	Colts	6	20
Matt Millen	Colts	4	19
Tedy Bruschi	Colts	4	18
Cris Carter	Colts	4	18
Herm Edwards	Colts	4	18
Merril Hoge	Colts	4	18
Chris McKendry	Colts	4	18

All 25 panelists picking the Colts were off by at best 18 points and at worst a staggering 29 points. On average, these 25 pundits underestimated the Saints by 22.32 points. Sure, anyone can make mistakes and pro football may be hard to predict, but having more than 2/3 of the expert panel be off by nearly ¼ of 100 points illustrates the lack of knowledge of or respect for the Saints.

Some interestingly poor predictions from the panel are listed below with game data to refute their claim.

"Peyton Manning does not throw 4th quarter interceptions." - Sal Paolantonio. Not only was Mr. Paolantonio's prediction of the game off by 25 points, but the only interception of the game was thrown by Peyton Manning in the 4th quarter.

"I feel a strong emotional pull towards the Saints but can't go against the best on the biggest stage, and Peyton is the gold standard." – Mike Tirico. What was this based upon? Brees beat Manning in nearly every QB category during the 2009 season. Why would previous seasons be more relevant than what is happening right now? Blind assessment of talent.

"Saints won't be able to keep up with Colts offense." - Mike Golic. The Saints were the #1 offense for 2009, and they outscored the Colts for 75% of the game covering the 2nd, 3rd, and 4th quarters. Another opinion not based on recent stats or possibly any stats at all.

"Colts, but Brees outplays Manning. Turnovers will hurt the Saints." - Colin Cowherd. Mr. Cowherd was half right. Brees did outplay Manning, which was a great call that took a lot of guts to make, but the Saints were perfect on turnovers, having none and forcing an interception off Manning. The Saints were #2 in the entire league in takeaways during the season, having 39 to the Green Bay Packers' 40. The Colts only had a meager 26 takeaways on the year, 18th in the league. The Saints had 39% more takeaways than giveaways, and the Colts only had 8% more takeaways than giveaways. Why would he think the Colts had the turnover advantage?

In other news, Peyton Manning was voted the league's MVP by a landslide vote, however, Drew Brees' key quarterback stats for the season were better in all but 1 of the important categories as shown in the chart at the top of the next page. Brees led the league with a phenomenal and record-breaking 70.6% completion ratio, a 109.6 QB Rating, 6.6 TD %, 8.3 Adjusted Net Yards Per Pass Attempt, and 34 touchdown passes.

The New Orleans Saints Story 103

Manning – Brees 2009 Regular Season Comparison

Leader is marked in **BOLD**

	TDs	Yards	Completion %	QB Rating	INT	ANY/A	TD %
Drew Brees	**34**	4,388	**70.6**	**109.6**	**11**	**8.3**	**6.6**
Peyton Manning	33	**4,500**	68.8	99.9	16	7.5	5.8

    Considering Brees' 70.6 completion % is a league record for the highest ever, the MVP voters should be ashamed of themselves for favoring the media darling and giving the award to Manning who was not the better quarterback this year. The voters clearly voted on hype and not statistics, as Manning only led in 1 of many categories (in the chart above, Brees cleanly beat Manning in 6 of 7 categories).

    The point being made here is not that Peyton Manning is a poor quarterback. Quite the contrary, Manning is an excellent quarterback who had a great year in 2009 and many others before that. The point of contention is that Brees had a better year in 2009, clearly proven in statistics, and was snubbed.

The Game Itself

Quarters	1	2	3	4	Total
Colts	10	0	7	0	17
Saints	0	6	10	15	31

1st Quarter: The Colts get on the board first with a 38-yard field goal from M. Stover. Indianapolis follows up the field goal with a Pierre Garcon 19-yard touchdown reception. At the end of the 1st quarter, the Saints trail the Colts 0-10.

2nd Quarter: The second quarter belongs entirely to the Saints, starting with a 46-yard Garrett Hartley field goal. The Colts' offense comes out for 3 plays and is sent back to the bench. The Saints drive down to the 1-yard line but are kept from scoring all the way through 4th down by the Colts defense. Then, the Saints send the Colts right back to the sidelines and end the quarter with another Hartley field goal from 44 yards out. The Saints defense holds the Indianapolis offense to no points, no 1st downs, and only 6 plays in the entire quarter, and they did so by sending the Colts 3 and out on their only 2 possessions. At the half, the Saints narrow the gap to 4 points, trailing the Colts 6-10.

3rd Quarter: The Saints start the 2nd half with an onside kick that was successfully recovered, which resulted in a 16-yard Drew Brees to Pierre Thomas touchdown reception, giving the Saints their first lead of the game at 13-10. The onside kick was also the 1st in Super Bowl history to occur before the 4th quarter. The Colts take the lead back with a 4-yard Addai rushing touchdown. Hartley kicks his 3rd field goal of the day, this one from 47 yards out. Hartley nailed 3 40+ yard field goals on the day to set a Super Bowl record. After 3 quarters, the Saints were behind by 1 with a score of 16-17.

4th Quarter: The 4th quarter belongs entirely to the Saints, who score on defense and offense while shutting out the Colts. The Colts miss a 51-yard Stover field goal attempt. The Saints scoring starts with a Jeremy Shockey 2-yard touchdown reception with a 2-point conversion scored by a nimble-footed Lance Moore. This score puts the Saints in the lead where they will stay for the rest of the contest. The Colts drive down the field but Peyton Manning is picked off by Tracy Porter who blazed down the field 74 yards for a New Orleans touchdown. The Colts drive down the field again, but are stopped by the New Orleans defense, allowing the Saints to take a knee to end the game as Super Bowl Champions. Final Score: Saints win 31-17.

GAME NOTES:

The Saints' defense, which was mocked by many commentators leading up to the game, kept the Colts scoreless for the 2nd and 4th quarters, only allowing 7 points total after the 1st quarter. They also generated the only interception of the game which was run back for a touchdown.

Brees was named Super Bowl MVP, validating his magnificent year.

Super Bowl Quarterback Comparison
Leader is marked in **BOLD**

	TDs	Yards	Completion%	QB Rating	INT	Completions
Drew Brees	**2**	288	**82.05**	**109.6**	**0**	**8.3**
Peyton Manning	0	**333**	68.88	99.9	1	7.5

It is notable to point out that Brees had 1 more completion than Manning on 6 less pass attempts, giving Brees a much superior pass rating for the Super Bowl.

15-3 Saints Record Going into the Super Bowl
16-3 Saints Record After the Super Bowl

Regular Season Reflections

Drew Brees led the league in many categories including a 70.6 completion ratio, 34 touchdowns, an 8.3 adjusted net yards per passing attempt, a 6.6 TD%, and a 109.6 passer rating. Brees had 4,388 yards during the regular season with only 11 interceptions.

On the ground, Pierre Thomas led the team with 793 rushing yards on 147 carries for 6 touchdowns and a 5.4 yards per carry average. Close behind was Mike Bell with 5 touchdowns and 654 yards on 172 carries with a 3.8 yards per carry average. Reggie Bush was third with 390 yards and 5 touchdowns on 70 carries with an average of 5.6 yards per carry.

Receiving rockets from Drew Brees was, first, Marquis Colston with 1,074 yards and 9 touchdowns on 70 receptions for a 15.3-yard average reception. Devery Henderson had 804 yards on 51 catches for 2 touchdowns and a 15.8-yard avg. Robert Meachem racked up 722 yards and 9 touchdowns on 45 catches. Popular among fans, Jeremy Shockey had 569 yards and 3 touchdowns on 48 grabs. The Saints had 4 receivers catching for over 550 yards, and 7 receivers who caught for over 300 yards.

On defense, Jonathan Vilma led in tackles with 87, followed by Roman Harper with 81. The interception king was Darren Sharper with 9. Next in line was Tracy Porter with 4. The team as a whole had 26 interceptions on the year. Will Smith led the team with 13 sacks, and the Saints had 35 sacks on the year as a whole.

John Carney was the leading scorer with 89 points. On the kicking front, Carney was 13 of 17 field goals for a 76.5%, and Garrett Hartley was 9 of 11 for an 81.8%.

Part III: Special Looks

JIM FINKS

No off-the-field member of the Saints organization is as well-known or appreciated by fans as Jim Finks.

Before becoming a part of the Saints organization in 1986, it is well known that the Saints had never had a winning season in its 19-year history in the NFL. But, what is not so well known is what Jim Finks had accomplished prior to his tenure in New Orleans.

Born in Missouri and having attended high school in Illinois, Finks went to The University of Tulsa, resulting in him being a 12th-round draft pick in 1949 by the Pittsburgh Steelers. As a player, Finks was both a quarterback and a defensive back, playing until 1955.

Following his retirement from play, he became an assistant coach at Notre Dame. Finks then moved to the Canadian Football League where he became general manager for the Calgary Stampeders, where he helped them achieve great success by scouting the best talent.

The NFL came calling for Finks in 1964 when the Minnesota Vikings named him as their general manager. By 1968, the Vikings won their first division and won 10 more divisional titles in the next 13 years. The talented defensive players that Finks scouted formed most of the legendary "Purple People Eaters." The Vikings made it to Super Bowl IV in 1970 (coincidentally held at Tulane Stadium in New Orleans) and Super Bowl VIII in 1974. For his work with The Vikings, Finks was named NFL Executive of the Year in 1973.

After resigning with the Vikings in 1974, Finks went to the Chicago Bears as general manager. Before Finks, the Bears had not reached the playoffs since 1963. Within 3 years, Finks had helped bring the Bears to the playoffs, and he did so again in 1979. With things looking upward for the Bears, it would seem Finks would have a long tenure there, but he resigned when Mike Ditka was hired as head coach by the team owner without Finks's approval in 1982. Strangely enough, Ditka would be named

Saints head coach in 1997, 3 years after Finks's death. Finks's contributions to The Bears were highly influential in their success throughout the 1980s, especially in their 1985 Super Bowl Championship.

Surprisingly after leaving the Bears, Finks stayed in Chicago, but he moved to Cubs baseball, working as President and CEO from 1983-1984, which included the Cubs becoming the 1984 National League Eastern Division Champs.

With so many years in football, it only made sense for Finks to return to the gridiron. This was when Jim Finks came to New Orleans in 1986. Finks's first key decision was to hire Jim Mora as head coach. In only Finks's second year with the long-suffering Saints, the team had its first winning season, going 12-3 and making their first appearance in the playoffs, losing to the Minnesota Vikings, the first team on which Finks had left his mark as a G.M. (note there were only 15 games in 1987 due to a player's strike). This season marked the second time Finks was named NFL Executive of the year.

Finks was rumored to be the likely successor as NFL Commissioner when Pete Rozelle retired in 1989. However, Paul Tagliabue was given the position.

Jim Finks died of lung cancer in 1994 in Metairie, LA, a suburb just outside of New Orleans, the last city whom he helped reinvigorate a love and belief in their football team.

Finks's legacy in the NFL is taking losing teams and turning them into postseason contenders. He had an eye for talent, and knew how to put the ingredients together into a championship caliber unit.

BUDDY DILIBERTO

Better known as Buddy D to the New Orleans area, Bernard Saverio Diliberto Jr. was born on August 18, 1931, in the Crescent City. He was a Saints TV/radio fixture going back to their first season, including work as a newspaper sports writer for *The Times Picayune*, a Saints radio show host on WWL, and sports director and anchor for local TV stations, ABC affiliate WVUE-TV channel 12 from 1966 to 1980 and NBC Affiliate WDSU-TV channel 6 from 1980-1990.

Buddy D is one of only 2 people discussed in depth in this book that were not players or coaches for the New Orleans Saints, the other being general manager Jim Finks. Simply being put in the same category as Jim Finks denotes a man that has contributed a great deal. The reason for this and what makes Diliberto notable is that mentioning Buddy D to anyone in the city of New Orleans will immediately bring the Saints to mind. Simply put, Buddy D is synonymous with The Saints, and any local would have a hard time discussing Mr. Diliberto and not mentioning the Black and Gold.

Buddy D embodied the hopes and the heartache that were experienced for so long by Saints' fans. There have truly been few other teams who can compare to the bad fortune endured by the Saints for so many years while still maintaining their fan base in the same city. Most other sports teams with similar records would have been long transplanted to another location. When most teams lose consistently, they become unprofitable quickly. Strangely enough, the Saints maintained a modest and loyal following even in their most despair-inducing years.

This is where Buddy D's special value to many Saints' fans came into play. His radio shows were often humorous, with Buddy D referring to insipid callers as "squirrels." He also made the proclamation that he would wear a dress if the Saints ever made it to the Super Bowl. He was a sounding board and someone who knew every bit of the bittersweet agony that his callers were feeling. His sense of humor could also help people cope with their negative feelings following the day's disaster on the gridiron. Knowing Buddy D was going to be back the next week as a Saints fan, gave cause for the listeners to stick around. In years when your team is 1-15, reasons to keep the faith are hard to come by.

Because Buddy D was so passionate, as many other Saints' fans are, he did have his detractors. Those who enjoyed him, loved him because he could vocalize their own frustrations, oftentimes in an extreme emotional fashion. This same trait is what others found unpleasing.

Prior to his sports career, Buddy Diliberto was awarded a Purple Heart for an injury he sustained during The Korean War. His sports-writing career began in 1950 writing for *The Times-Picayune* newspaper in New Orleans as a student at Loyola University.

Diliberto popularized/originated many bits of Saints culture, such as the moniker "The Aints" and fans wearing brown paper bags over their heads.

One of Diliberto's most famous quotes is, "When you go to Heaven after you die, tell St. Peter you're a Saints fan. He'll say, 'C'mon in, I don't care what else you done, you suffered enough.'"

The biggest controversy in Diliberto's long career goes back to January of 1986. Super Bowl XX between the flashy Chicago Bears and the New England Patriots was set in New Orleans. Jim McMahon, William "The Refrigerator" Perry, Walter Payton, and crew were a very high profile team that garnered many fans and many detractors. The team recorded a rap song, "The Super Bowl Shuffle" just before their Super Bowl XX appearance, and the song made it to #41 on the Billboard U.S. Charts. The video for the song included the team and was also quite popular on MTV. While many thought the song to be arrogant, including Bears' own Dan Hampton who refused to participate, the profits were given to charity. To their credit, the Bears had an amazing year with a 15-1 record plus winning the Super Bowl.

Public enemy #1 for the Bears' haters was quarterback Jim McMahon. McMahon was seen more often wearing Tom Cruise-style sunglasses than without, and he was an interviewer's dream, rarely being found without a colorful or controversial comment. At his first press event as a Bear, McMahon arrived drinking a beer. At times, he was involved in conflict with head coach Mike Ditka, teammates, and the press. On a team criticized as being too flashy, McMahon was the most flamboyant, which made him the focal point for criticism.

In all fairness, McMahon's sunglasses were a medical necessity from an eye injury he sustained as a child, which is why he had a tinted visor in his football helmet.

All of this anti-Bears sentiment played a part in the controversy with Diliberto. Buddy D's Saints were 5-11 in 1985 and still had never had a winning season. It's not hard to envision a longtime fan of such a team having disdain for a brash, super-cocky 15-1 Chicago Bears team that were not only in the Super Bowl, but were likely to win it in the Saints' home of the Superdome. None of the above has been proven to be Buddy D's motivation, but it is a suggestion as to what he may have been feeling.

Furthermore, the *Times-News* in Henderson, N.C., reported on January 24th, 1986, that Jim McMahon had recently argued with his Bears management to get them to fly out an acupuncturist to massage his bruised buttocks, was on Bourbon Street playing the role of the Pied Piper, and mooned a helicopter leading up to Super Bowl XX. McMahon was certainly not trying to endear himself to anyone.

Days before the Super Bowl, Buddy D claimed that Jim McMahon had called the men and women of New Orleans "idiots" and "sluts." Buddy's exact words were: (pg 21 *Times-News*)

> "Jim McMahon apparently, on a radio interview with WLS, the Chicago radio station, really ripped New Orleans. He ripped the people, he ripped the ladies, he ripped a lot of things.
> Basically, I understand, he said most of the ladies he ran into were sluts. He said most of the people he ran into were stupid. And things like that. And they said he really took off."

Special Looks 114

Dozens of New Orleanians protested outside the Bears' Super Bowl Headquarters, and there were claims of anonymous death threats. Jim McMahon denied ever making the comments, joking that he would never be awake early enough to be on the radio show on which he was accused of making the comments. There was no evidence to prove McMahon had said anything, and he was indeed not interviewed at all on WLS that week. Diliberto and WDSU apologized for the erroneous comments, and Diliberto was suspended for 2 weeks.

Diliberto's exact apology was, "I sincerely apologize for the problems caused by these unverified statements. I wish Jim McMahon and the Bears well in the Super Bowl Sunday and hope the remainder of the week is devoted to preparations for the game without distractions caused by my comments last night." (pg 21 *Times-News*)

Buddy D did return to his job after the brief suspension and covered the Saints through 2005.

Fast forward to 2010, 5 years after Diliberto's passing, and one of his most memorable sayings has come to the forefront. The New Orleans Saints have made it to the Super Bowl. Shouldn't someone be wearing a dress?

Buddy Diliberto's replacement as radio sportscaster on the Saints after-game show was none other than Bobby Hebert, the quarterback who led the Saints to their first winning seasons. To honor his predecessor, The Cajun Canon Hebert took up Buddy D's vow to wear a dress in a parade spanning from the Super Dome to the French Quarter in downtown New Orleans.

According to Diliberto tribute website Buddy's Broads, Bobby's exact words following the Saints' victory over the Brett Farve-led Vikings to get into the Super Bowl were, "The freaking Saints are going to the Superbowl! Hell ya! We going to Miami, baby. It was the Saints (sic) destiny to go the the Superbowl. The Who Dat Nation deserves this win! In honor of Buddy D, hell yes, I'm wearing a dress!" (http://www.buddysbroads.com/)

A doctored photo of Buddy D wearing a dress was printed in New Orleans newspaper, *The Times-Picayune*. The photo was well-received, reminding fans of both Diliberto's long service and how far the team has come.

SAINTS HEAD COACHES BY YEAR

Coach	Years	Games	Win %	Won	Lost	Tie
Tom Fears	1967-1970	49	.277	13	34	2
J. D. Roberts	1970-1972	35	.219	7	25	3
John North	1973-1975	34	.324	11	23	N/A
Ernie Hefferle	1975	8	.125	1	7	N/A
Hank Stram	1976-1977	28	.250	7	21	N/A
Dick Nolan	1978-1980	44	.341	15	29	N/A
Dick Stanfel	1980	4	.250	1	3	N/A
Bum Phillips	1981-1985	69	.391	27	42	N/A
Wade Phillips	1985	4	.250	1	3	N/A
Jim Mora	1986-1996	167	.557	93	74	N/A
Rick Venturi	1996	8	.125	1	7	N/A
Mike Ditka	1997-1999	48	.313	15	33	N/A
Jim Haslett	2000-2005	96	.469	45	51	N/A
Sean Payton	2006-2009	64	.594	38	26	N/A

Saints Head Coaches by Win %

Win %	Coach	Won	Lost	Tie
.594	Sean Payton	38	26	N/A
.557	Jim Mora	93	74	N/A
.469	Jim Haslett	45	51	N/A
.391	Bum Phillips	27	42	N/A
.341	Dick Nolan	15	29	N/A
.324	John North	11	23	N/A
.313	Mike Ditka	15	33	N/A
.277	Tom Fears	13	34	2
.250	Hank Stram	7	21	N/A
.250	Dick Stanfel	1	3	N/A
.250	Wade Phillips	1	3	N/A
.219	J. D. Roberts	7	25	3
.125	Ernie Hefferle	1	7	N/A
.125	Rick Venturi	1	7	N/A

Head Coaches by Saints Games Coached

Games Coached	Coach	Years
167	Jim Mora	1986-1996
96	Jim Haslett	2000-2005
69	Bum Phillips	1981-1985
64	Sean Payton	2006-2009
48	Mike Ditka	1997-1999
44	Dick Nolan	1978-1980
35	J. D. Roberts	1970-1972
34	John North	1973-1975

28	Hank Stram	1976-1977
8	Ernie Hefferle	1975
8	Rick Venturi	1996
4	Dick Stanfel	1980
4	Wade Phillips	1985

Special Looks 118

SAINTS COACHING AWARDS

Tom Fears
Pro Football Hall of Fame

Hank Stram
Pro Football Hall of Fame

Jim Mora
Associated Press NFL Coach of the Year 1987
Pro Football Weekly NFL Coach of the Year 1987
The Sporting News NFL Coach of the Year 1987
UPI NFL Coach of the Year 1987

Mike Ditka
Pro Football Hall of Fame

Jim Haslett
Associated Press NFL Coach of the Year 2000
Pro Football Weekly NFL Coach of the Year 2000

Sean Payton
Associated Press NFL Coach of the Year 2006
Maxwell Football Club NFL Coach of the Year 2006
Pro Football Weekly NFL Coach of the Year 2006
The Sporting News NFL Coach of the Year 2006
Maxwell Football Club NFL Coach of the Year 2009
The Sporting News NFL Coach of the Year 2009

SAINTS QUARTERBACKS BY YEAR
Number of Games Played *in Italics* Next to the Player's Name

1967   Gary Cuozzo *10* – Billy Kilmer *4*
1968   Billy Kilmer *11* – Karl Sweetan *2* – Ronnie Lee South *1*
1969   Billy Kilmer *16*
1970   Billy Kilmer *11* – Ed Hargett *3*
1971   Archie Manning *10* – Ed Hargett *4*
1972   Archie Manning *14*
1973   Archie Manning *13* – Bobby Scott *1*
1974   Archie Manning *11* – Larry Cipa *2* – Bobby Scott *1*
1975   Archie Manning *13* – Larry Cipa *1*
1976   Bobby Scott *8* – Bobby Douglass *6*
1977   Archie Manning *9* – Bobby Scott *3* – Bobby Douglass *2*
1978   Archie Manning *16*
1979   Archie Manning *16*
1980   Archie Manning *16*
1981   Archie Manning *11* – Dave Wilson *4* – Bobby Scott *1*
1982   Ken Stabler *8* – Guido Merkens *1*
1983   Ken Stabler *14* – Dave Wilson *2*
1984   Richard Todd *14* – Dave Wilson *2*
1985   Dave Wilson *10* – Bobby Hebert *6*
1986   Dave Wilson *13* – Bobby Hebert *3*
1987   Bobby Hebert *12* – John Fourcade *3*
1988   Bobby Hebert *16*
1989   Bobby Hebert *13* – John Fourcade *3*
1990   Steve Walsh *11* – John Fourcade *5*
1991   Bobby Hebert *9* – Steve Walsh *7*
1992   Bobby Hebert *16*
1993   Wade Wilson *14* – Mike Buck *1* – Steve Walsh *1*
1994   Jim Everett *16*
1995   Jim Everett *16*
1996   Jim Everett *15* – Doug Nussmeier *1*
1997   Heath Shuler *9* – Billy Joe Hobert *4* – Danny Wuerffel *2* – Doug Nussmeier *1*

1998 Kerry Collins *7* – Danny Wuerffel *4* – Billy Joe Tolliver *4* – Billy Joe Hobert *1*
1999 Billy Joe Tolliver *7* – Billy Joe Hobert *7* – Jake Delhomme *2*
2000 Jeff Blake *11* – Aaron Brooks *5*
2001 Aaron Brooks *16*
2002 Aaron Brooks *16*
2003 Aaron Brooks *16*
2004 Aaron Brooks *16*
2005 Aaron Brooks *13* – Todd Bouman *3*
2006 Drew Brees *16*
2007 Drew Brees *16*
2008 Drew Brees *16*
2009 Drew Brees *15* – Mark Brunell *1*

Top 10 All-Time Saints Passing Yard Leaders

Rank	Player	Yards	Years
1	Archie Manning	21,734	1971-1975, 1977-1981
2	Aaron Brooks	19,156	2000-2005
3	Drew Brees	18,298	2006-2009
4	Bobby Hebert	14,630	1985-1989, 1991-1992
5	Jim Everett	10,622	1994-1996
6	Billy Kilmer	7,490	1967-1970
7	Dave Wilson	6,987	1981, 1983-1986
8	Steve Walsh	3,879	1990-1991, 1993
9	Kenny Stabler	3,670	1982-1983
10	Billy Joe Tolliver	3,343	1998-1999

Top 10 Saints Season Passing Yard Leaders

Rank	Quarterback	Yards	Year
1	Drew Brees	5,069	2008
2	Drew Brees	4,423	2007

3	Drew Brees	4,418	2006
4	Drew Brees	4,388	2009
5	Jim Everett	3,970	1995
6	Jim Everett	3,855	1994
7	Aaron Brooks	3,832	2001
8	Aaron Brooks	3,810	2004
9	Archie Manning	3,716	1980
10	Aaron Brooks	3,572	2002

Top 10 Saints Season Passer Rating Leaders

Rank	Quarterback	Passer Rating	Year
1	Drew Brees	109.6	2009
2	Drew Brees	96.2	2008
3	Drew Brees	96.2	2006
4	John Fourcade	92.0	1989
5	Drew Brees	89.4	2007
6	Aaron Brooks	88.8	2003
7	Jim Everett	87.0	1995
8	Aaron Brooks	85.7	2000
9	Jim Everett	84.9	1994
10	Dave Wilson	83.9	1984

Total Career Regular Season Games Played with Saints

Games	Player	Years
129	Archie Manning	1971-1975, 1977-1981
82	Aaron Brooks	2000-2005
75	Bobby Hebert	1985-1989, 1991-1992
63	Drew Brees	2006-2009
47	Jim Everett	1994-1996
42	Billy Kilmer	1967-1970
31	Dave Wilson	1981, 1983-1986

Special Looks 122

22	Ken Stabler	1982-1983
19	Steve Walsh	1990-1991, 1993
14	Bobby Scott	1973-1974, 1976-1977, 1981
14	Richard Todd	1984
14	Wade Wilson	1993
12	Billy Joe Hobert	1997-1999
11	John Fourcade	1987, 1989-1990
11	Gary Cuozzo	1967
11	Billy Joe Tolliver	1998-1999
11	Jeff Blake	2000
10	Gary Cuozzo	1967
9	Heath Shuler	1997
8	Bobby Douglass	1976-1977
7	Ed Hargett	1970-1971
7	Kerry Collins	1998
6	Danny Wuerffel	1997-1998
3	Larry Cipa	1974-1975
3	Todd Bouman	2005
2	Karl Sweetan	1968
2	Doug Nussmeier	1996-1997
2	Jake Delhomme	1999
1	Mark Brunell	2009
1	Guido Merkens	1982
1	Mike Buck	1993
1	Ronnie Lee South	1968

Top 10 Saints CAREER Passing Touchdown Leaders

Rank	Player	Career Touchdowns as a Saint
1	Drew Brees	122
2	Aaron Brooks	120
3	Archie Manning	115
4	Bobby Hebert	85
5	Jim Everett	60
6	Billy Kilmer	47
7	Dave Wilson	36
8	Steve Walsh	25

9	Kenny Stabler	17
10	Bobby Scott	15

Top 10 Saints SEASON Passing Touchdown Leaders

Rank	Quarterback	Passing TD's	Year
1 (tie)	Drew Brees	34	2009
1 (tie)	Drew Brees	34	2008
2	Drew Brees	28	2007
3	Aaron Brooks	27	2002
4	Drew Brees	26	2006
5	Jim Everett	26	1995
6	Aaron Brooks	26	2001
7	Aaron Brooks	24	2003
8	Archie Manning	23	1980
9	Jim Everett	22	1994

Lightning Source UK Ltd.
Milton Keynes UK
UKHW011437010219
336576UK00010B/788/P